Mediamobiles

Views from the Road

The Public Library

REPORTER

Number 19

Mediamobiles:

Views from the Road

Edited by

Don Roberts

with

Deirdre Boyle

65

AMERICAN LIBRARY ASSOCIATION

CHICAGO 1979

Library of Congress Cataloging in Publication Data

Main entry under title:

Mediamobiles : views from the road.

  (Public library reporter ; no. 19)
  Bibliography: p.
  Includes index.
  1. Bookmobiles--United States. I. Roberts,
Don, 1931-   II. Boyle, Deirdre. III. Series.
Z671.P25 no. 19 [Z686] 027.4'05s [027.4'73]
ISBN 0-8389-3232-0   79-18488

Printed in the United States of America

Contents

iv Contents

Preface

A few years ago, when library buildings and services were being integrated and library media vehicles had just started to roll, no one really thought of including this new aspect of library service in their master plans. The vans kept moving and the mediamobilers had few opportunities to exchange information. Many people entered the field without being aware that similar services were available elsewhere. Most information was passed on by word of mouth.

About four years ago Marvin Scilken, the former chairperson of the Public Library Association Editorial Committee, suggested a Public Library Reporter on mediamobiles. We quickly found that one of the problems with naming something is that the name remains, even as the creation changes; thus today's media vehicle is often still called a bookmobile.

A library media vehicle is not a bookmobile; instead it contains sophisticated electrical and electronic devices such as video, a two-way radio, and a telephone. It can deliver and show communications formats other than print, although it often includes microprint as well, and it can receive and record both audio and video messages.

This study considers five types of media vehicles:

    1. A fully integrated vehicle that can deliver and show media software. Two examples cited

here are operated by the Berkeley Public Library in California and by Portland Public Library in Maine.

2. A vehicle that is designed to hold meetings, presentations, and events as well as deliver and show media software. Examples in the study are Weston Woods vehicles and the Readily Accessible Materials Van at Buffalo/Erie County Library in Buffalo, New York.

3. A vehicle that can produce media as well as show and deliver software. Indiana's Vigo County Library has a mediamobile built by Gerstenslager that demonstrates this type.

4. A vehicle that only makes presentations, such as puppet shows, films, and story hours. The mobile unit run by Daniel Boone Regional Library in Columbia, Missouri, represents this category.

5. An information vehicle that utilizes telephones including video phones, computer hookups, micrographics, and photocopy machines instead of the more conventional media software and hardware. Such a vehicle has been built and operated by the New York Telephone Company.

In addition to these is the modified bookmobile. This is a traditional book delivery vehicle that has added something to its services--a record player, film projector, microfiche reader, or an audio amplifier with outside speakers to attract the public. Since AM/FM radios have been in use for years, they cannot be considered as anything more than a bookmobile modification at this point.

The Introduction, a brief historical survey of library vehicle services, presents some of the key problems and issues threading through the interviews that follow. These conversations are with some of the men and women who represent the first media generation to follow the "books on wheels" models. Some, in designing their vehicles and services, have taken important risks, while others have simply modified the basic bookmobile. Their stories will help in the designing and running of efficient, imaginative, and integrated library vehicles. Don Roberts conducted the interviews between 1972 and 1973. They were reviewed again before publication. These interviews have been grouped around manufacture of vehicles, an organization intended to invite close comparisons and analysis of media vehicle experiences.

Some Afterthoughts follow the interviews with recommendations for the future, including Toward Guidelines for Mobile Library Service. The appendix includes vehicle specifications for some of the units described in the interviews. The bibliography was compiled by George A. Plosker; Sanford Berman compiled the index.

There are many people we would like to thank for their help in producing this Reporter. We are grateful to the mediamobile people who took time to share their thoughts, plans, and problems. Marvin Scilken had the idea for this issue and Syd Popinski, who took over as PLA Editorial Committee chairperson, has seen it through to completion. Morton Schindel was particularly helpful in getting the project moving. Thanks also to Inelda Thompson, Jan Roberts, and James (Jay) Johnstone, to the Hennepin County Library and the Public Library Association staff at ALA headquarters.

Introduction

A few years from now we will celebrate the centennial anniversary of the first hitching of a library cart to an internal combustion engine. Except
for a few improvements such as air conditioning,
electronic ignitions, and suspension systems, our
current version of the library's horseless carriage
hasn't changed much since 1902.
By 2002 media vans could be well behind us, replaced by a vehicle that features the most advanced
technology able to deliver messages in all the dom-
inant information formats of the day. This twenty-
first century vehicle will be sophisticated, flexible, and economical. Our task today is to decide
how to make this vision possible and how to design
and use the vehicles we have now so that we can
survive the funding and information crises that lie
ahead.
Our antecedents stretch back to the Roman roads,
the Viking sea lanes, smoke signals, and the pony
express routes. A century ago this nation of immi-
grants agreed, along with Andrew Carnegie, to store
and use public information in buildings and to have
vehicles deliver selected printed documents to homes
and institutions. These vehicles were thought to be
useful only for as long as the recipients lived in
unincorporated areas or were otherwise unable to
afford architectural answers to their information
problems. The American Library Association produced

elaborate and ambitious plans to construct libraries throughout the country that would be located at convenient distances from each other. This plan would eventually have phased out vehicles except in some rural areas.

More sophisticated information delivery systems and changing economic considerations, such as limits to growth, have shown us the inappropriateness of library building proliferation. It is time to scrap the notion that links vehicles to library expansion. We must view library mobile units as important in themselves, as integral parts of local, state, national, and international information services.

At the turn of the century, the possibility of mobile services depended upon the portability of books. With portability a continuing consideration, bookmobiles today usually carry paperbacks and microfiche readers, offering hardbound books only upon request.

Vehicles do not have their own collections: they are dependent upon the library building's resources. Just as print has dominated the design and use of library architecture, so has it extended to library vehicles. Another reason for the slow addition of media has been the weight factor. Early models for both hardware and software were heavy. With the development and standardization of tape and integrated circuitry, smaller and lighter mediaware became available. With the weight reduction due to lighter book loads, room has been made for light and portable media software like audio cassettes and phonograph records.

The road is a romantic part of American mythology. Conversations with bookmobile librarians and their crews reflect this romance, and it is tempting to get sidetracked by stories about "the time we got stuck on the shoulder in the blizzard." Then there are the survival tales on how to keep that 15-year-old relic off its frame or how to appease the library director and board who are complaining about that one-way, 30-mile trip to deliver a handful of books to one family. And don't forget the plots to get that moldy vehicle replaced by a new one. As engrossing as these stories are, bookmobiling literature is dominated by writings that essentially ignore communications issues. Romantic fervor does nothing to obviate the need for

up-to-date solutions to such problems as setting
standards or guidelines for equipment, maintenance,
and personnel; developing long-range plans for mobile service that match those for production units
operated by TV network affiliates; and exploring
ways to influence equipment manufacturers.

In order to innovate with media vehicles, the
librarian must obtain funds and these must be voted
by the library director and the library board. But
these people are often out of touch with the library's constituency and unable to perceive the
needs of the public. They deny support for vehicle
improvements and service, preferring instead to
construct or modify library buildings.

As long as the people who make the final deci-
sions on major expenditures consider buildings
first and vehicles second, we cannot hope for progress. Further, if library administrators and
boards continue to follow the thinking of the ar-
chitects and bookmobile builders they hire, design
progress will not be made. All mobile library service today depends upon standardized truck and bus
chassis, and they are part of the problem.

Step into a brand new bookmobile in 1978, and
you will find a miniature library complete with
books, charging machine, an electric fan, and a
bulletin board. The people who planned and paid for
this vehicle apparently do not know that there may
be other models to work from. Yesterday's designs
cannot satisfy today's service needs. Buckminster
Fuller, among others, has pointed out over and over
again that we cannot design solutions for the present based on past models; an airplane will be less
efficient if it is modeled on a train.

The solution to our vehicular problems will
come from radical, integrative innovations. Design
will have to get away from what has been called the
"edifice complex" and deal with the real problems
of transience and communication. Mobility patterns
will change many times between now and the one hun-
dred anniversary of the mechanization of our library service. It is up to us to keep our minds
open and be willing to push ahead and experiment
if we are to solve these problems and justify our
continuance. The following section provides a set
of recommendations designed to facilitate the establishment of a practical and efficient mobile library service.

TOWARD GUIDELINES FOR MOBILE LIBRARY SERVICE

Rising costs of fuel and labor on custom instal-
lations further complicate the problem of setting
guidelines for mobile services. The indifference of
bookmobile manufacturers to the problem of gasoline
consumption, for example, is only one of many indi-
cations that standards and guidelines for future mobile vehicles will not come from the manufacturers.
We must initiate the guidelines and must do it quickly if mobile delivery and production vehicles are to
survive at all in library service.

The recommendations that follow are based upon
three assumptions:

1. The bookmobile is a product of obsolete technology: it lacks integrity and does not work
   well.
2. Mobile services are an essential part of library service networks. To justify their continuance, mobile vehicles must expand their
   operations. Their equipment must work better
   and be more cost-effective.
3. To serve current needs, mobile services must
   have proper vehicles that can deliver information in appropriate formats and, when software is not available, produce information
   requested by the public.

Design Recommendations

Design is the key to future mobile services.
Eugene Healy, in an article on bookmobiles written
in 1971 (see bibliography for complete citation),
called upon manufacturers to employ design staffs
that could accommodate individual library requirements in their designs along with the latest ad-
vances in space and aeronautic design, especially
regarding weight, electronics, and safety. At that
time a Gerstenslager representative wrote that,
"on review of this article, it has been determined
that the bookmobile proposed would . . . cost at
least $150,000." Considering the dollars spent on
other vehicular development (e.g., space vehicles,
or compact automobiles like Volkswagen's "Rabbit")
the price for development seems very small. The
automotive industry, given sufficient resources by
agencies like The Department of Health, Education,

and Welfare (HEW), could solve many design and production problems.

Healy's article is a good place to start in compiling design guidelines. Some new recommendations can be added to those he made.

Mobile Services Guidelines should include:

1. Vehicle compliance with all safety standards set by states for school buses.
2. Power-to-weight-to-fuel consumption ratios.
3. Chassis requirements that insure that springs, shocks, steering mechanisms, and the like will hold up and adjust to terrain, parking, and other factors.
4. Automatic inclusion of automotive improvements as they occur: e.g., electronic ignitions, disc brakes, and position of engines in relation to drive wheels.
5. Performance requirements for generators and other automotive equipment; specifics should be based on the demands made on equipment and should include guidelines for durability (i.e., warranties).
6. Access to all moving parts of the vehicle to permit adjustments, cleaning, and repair.
7. Use of lightweight metal and fiberglass instead of plywood in construction for added durability and lightness.
8. Design that permits both the storage, presentation, and production of audiovisual materials.
9. Modular design that allows for the exchange of equipment to accommodate varying needs.
10. Design of electric and electronic components that permits adjustments and updating as innovations occur: e.g., the replacement or addition of a video cassette system with a video disc system.
11. Design to permit access by handicapped persons.
12. A list of basic components for all vehicles that might include: an all-purpose amplifier; inside and outside speakers; AM/FM radio; audio cassette players; antennae for radio and TV; and—whenever possible—radio-telephone units, mini photocopiers, and microfiche readers.

Additional recommendations can be found in the interviews, and readers will undoubtedly come up with further suggestions. Final guidelines should not be limited to the familiar four-, six-, and eight-wheel vehicles powered by either internal combustion or diesel engines. These guidelines should keep in mind visionary library mobile services by trains, boats, information satellites, and other vehicles.

A Basic Proposal

The Public Library Association must exert leadership in mobile library service by convening a preconference on the survival and expansion of mobile services. Representatives from all states and manufacturers should be invited. A task force should be appointed to prepare guidelines, make recommendations, and devise a plan to implement them. The results could then be taken to the main conference in a program for the entire membership that would dramatize the possible extinction of mobile services and encourage the adoption of this "orphan" library service. As we chart the future of libraries, "media machines" must figure prominently in the blueprints for tomorrow's information services.

Conversations with Media Vehicle Pioneers

MARONEY

Bob Maroney

"The trend is away from 10 percent media and 90 percent print into, let's say, 60 percent print and 40 percent media. When I say media, I'm including children's games, arts, and crafts programs—things that the traditional New England Yankee wouldn't call 'library programs,' but would consider school projects."

DR: Where do you see design going beyond the book-mobile stage? So often the media vehicles are simply "media-ized" bookmobiles. I'm concerned with innovative approaches and some of the things that you think are extensions beyond what has already been done. I'm also interested in your comments on the energy crunch and how you are going to relate to the manufacturers in terms of the economy of these vehicles.

BM: We might as well start with the Portland Book-mobile. That started out, as I understand it, as a regular bookmobile and then was adapted into a media-mobile to serve the handicapped. With the combination of an elevator, rear projection screen, total sound system, and removable shelves that hide desks equipped with electrical outlets and wider doors, the

handicapped could be served. Going from a standard
27-inch wide door to a 33-inch wide door allows the
use of a ramp and/or elevator in a given area. From
what I have seen, it has been a very successful project.

Now six or seven other libraries want to design
dual-purpose machines like the one in Portland. They
primarily want the same thing, although some may
want to go to a different sound system or a different type of audiovisual setup. One bookmobile had a
projection room in the back of it. It was a standard
bookmobile except for the back ten feet, which had a
separate sound projection room. You could project
either outside of the vehicle via a rear projection
screen or in the vehicle with a rear projection
screen and pull down screen located at the front of
the bookmobile. This way children would be able to
sit inside during inclement weather.

DR: Who built that?

BM: We built it for the Washington County Library
System in Greenville, Mississippi. They wanted to
advertise the bookmobile to the people of Washington
County so that everyone would be aware of everything
it could do and would make use of the services.
There was a little article in American Libraries on
it. The Central Massachusetts Regional Library System, based in Worcester, just got a regional bookmobile. The normal bookmobile carries 2,500 volumes,
print only. They are going into perhaps half that
number in books so that the lower half of the interior space can be built for projectors, screens,
films, cassettes, videotape equipment, posters, and
framed art prints. It will also serve a dual purpose. This particular vehicle does not serve the
population per se. It serves the libraries. Its pri-
mary function is not going house-to-house, but
library-to-library, so that the library in the re-
gion can borrow from the bookmobile without waiting
two or more days. This is adaptable and could be
used on a standard patron stop arrangement. If you
had six projectors on a bookmobile at all times, a
person could theoretically go into the bookmobile,
look around, find a film that he liked, and borrow
the film, projector, and screen. The one drawback
is that equipment is so expensive you would have to
have a great deal of it. A lot of libraries are

hesitant to do this because of tight fiscal programs. But this is a possibility.

We are in the planning stages of
a total, "100% mediamobile" in Ocean   100%
City, New Jersey, which is currently   Mediamobile
stalled because of lack of funding.
Their intention is to set up a mediamobile in theater-style. There would
be room for approximately 40 people
to sit inside the mediamobile and see
a film, listen to a story hour, see a puppet show,
and so forth. In addition to that, a 4 x 8-foot panel inside the vehicle could be used to put a full-
scale movie on outside with appropriate sound equipment to go along with it. This is a project that's
in limbo now because of a tight fiscal situation.

The trend is away from 10 percent media and 90
percent print into, let's say, 60 percent print and
40 percent media. When I say media, I'm including
children's games, arts, and crafts programs—things
that the traditional New England Yankee wouldn't
call "library programs," but would consider school
projects.

DR: When I talk to other companies they say
they'll do anything the school or library wants.
They don't try to feed the customer ideas. When you
communicate with a client, do you suggest innovations to them? Do you set certain standards? For
example, do you recommend that they have radio communications so that they can hear weather reports?

BM: If someone calls up and says, "I want a bookmobile but I want to be able to show movies on it.
What is your suggestion?" I come up with a list of
mobiles that have done this in the past, such as
the Portland bookmobile and mediamobile combination.
We are the only ones to build only bookmobiles, so
we must maintain our reputation. We live and die on
bookmobiles and associated equipment such as mediamobiles. If a customer says to me, "What do we need?"
I'll look at his traffic flow, look at his bookmobiles, discuss what the problems are, and what
should have been on it that wasn't included. Then
I'll take a combination of his ideas and our ideas,
as far as the body is concerned, and come up with
a set of specifications to meet his needs.

Regardless of whether the customer buys the

chassis or the complete unit with us supplying the chassis, we will come up with a set of recommended chassis specifications. After they have had a chance to look at them, we will go to the local dealer and say, "What do you think of these specifications?" The local dealer knows the terrain, knows the mileage, knows everything about what that bookmobile is going to do. We look at past repair expenses over a period of years. Were the brakes or the springs too small? Was the generator a problem because local service wasn't available? We try to come up with a unit that will spend as many hours as possible on the road and as few hours as possible in the garage.

When the bookmobile is ready to be delivered, somebody from the company, usually myself, gets behind the wheel and drives it to the library. This gives us the opportunity to shake the thing down prior to delivery. God knows, as long as there are human beings involved in the manufacturing of anything, there can be troubles. So we test out our bookmobiles under road conditions.

Testing under Road Conditions

After the bookmobile is delivered, we do something that is unique. We spend as much time as necessary to go over the bookmobile with the customer, the staff, the director, the mechanic from the garage that services the chassis, and the mechanic that services the generator so that everybody is thoroughly familiar with the unit. You have to know your customers. You have to know what they want and what they are thinking. You have to engineer conservatively to meet their needs. Let's say it's a southern climate and they want air conditioning. We come up with an air conditioning system that has been proven adequate in past bookmobiles for that climate. Let's say we decide on a 36,000 BTU air conditioner. A 10kw generator would run the system while a 7½kw generator would also run it, but not very well. We try to build a power reserve into the bookmobile so that if the system calls for precisely 10kws, we provide a 12½kw generator. We want a generator that will run that air conditioner next year, five years from now, and ten years from now, provided that a preventive maintenance program is followed. If you need a 20,000 pound gross vehicle weight rating, buy a 25,000 pound or 27,000 pound, because bookmobiles are completely different in design from any other truck. A bookmobile carries its full load 365 days a year. It carries this load not in the center, as the normal truck does, but on the outside walls. The weight factor on the bookmobile will vary plus or minus 500 pounds in any given day, and it will never run empty nor will it ever run completely full. All of these things have to be taken into account when you make a recommendation to a library.

There are three different styles of bookmobiles. We make recommendations as to the style of bookmobile that we think the customer should have for reasons of serviceability, maintenance, and local service. If they have a good working relationship with an International Harvester garage, we might recommend an International chassis. If they have only a Chevrolet garage in town, we will sell a Chevrolet chassis, or we'll strongly suggest they buy the Chevrolet for the local service. This is probably the single most important factor in the whole bookmobile purchase. What components are you putting into it? Where are you getting service? If the bookmobile must be driven 200 miles to get its engine tuned up, ten hours are wasted.

When the bookmobile is delivered, a complete maintenance handbook comes with it. There is a separate page for a driver to use every day. He goes out and checks certain things off on a prescribed form, signs his name to it, puts the odometer reading down, the hourly reading for the generator, etc. That form is sent to the director so the people in charge of the operation will know what is being done. Even a driver who really doesn't care must fill out the form to keep his job. This will help to prove if he is at fault, because if there is no oil in the bookmobile and he drives away with it, he has certified that there is no oil in it. It helps to pin down responsibility.

Preventive maintenance is the most important aspect of a bookmobile. Once you have the vehicle, you must take care of it. People think that it is very expensive to take care of, but it's not.

Preventive Maintenance

DR: How do you stress communications?

BM: There are many ways of communicating between bookmobile and library. You have to take into account that some communication systems are [initially] very expensive and continue to be expensive year after year. Our theory on a bookmobile is that it should be just one separate room of the library, offering everything that the library offers. The bookmobile has always been a step-child to the library. Get people interested in the library via the bookmobile and you will hopefully get them coming to the library as an advertising arrangement.

One library I know does reference by telephone. They have a mobile telephone in the bookmobile; they invite reference questions and then call the reference department at the library. If it's a fairly simple thing, the reference librarian will answer the question on the spot. If it's involved, the reference librarian will go over it, find the information, make up a reader's list and send it to this person. The person can get some kind of answer immediately. This is one of the most important things. By using these telephones, they also run a book-by-mail program. If a patron comes in and wants a particular book and the book is not available on the bookmobile, a phone call is made to the main library to see if it's there. If the book is there and a patron cannot get to the library, the library will put the book in a book bag, address it, and send it to the patron. The patron will return it to the main library or to the bookmobile. Or he can mail it, if he wishes.

In some libraries, the two-way radio-telephone came into use because old bookmobiles were breaking down in remote and dangerous places. The radio-telephone was added in so that if the unit got a flat tire or had a group of kids trying to vandalize the outside of the truck, the staff could call a garage or the police. A couple of libraries have put in dummy telephones which do not work and are not hooked up to anything but simply give them a psychological advantage over someone who thinks of doing something he shouldn't be doing. The least expensive form of emergency communications is the citizens' band radio. A complete system costs $500 plus the license.

Two-way Radio Communications

DR: No reference?

BM: Well, CB radio, as you may know, can be used for reference questions. CB is legitimate business communications equipment. The major problem with the CB radio is that there are so many people who have it and so many people on different channels. You can get a CB radio now with 23 channels. The library may choose to monitor channel 1, for instance; if it is busy while the library is trying to get the bookmobile or the bookmobile is trying to get the library, the operator can stand by while the other searches through 40 channels to find a channel that is not being used, then go back to channel 1, tell the other person to go to channel 21 or whatever, and do a brief reference check. The two-way radio-telephone is probably the best and most private way of doing such research. The CB radio will get the job done but there are lots of problems. If you have the money to spend, you can hook up with the city, county, or state radio system.

DR: Civil defense?

BM: There's the civil defense network, or you can hook up with the police or fire department radio— a place where there is someone on the other end of the line 24 hours a day. That is good for an emergency, but not good for reference or mail-a-book.

DR: Has anyone approached you to have a vehicle that could be stripped inside and used for library media production—say for video products?

BM: You're talking about having sides open up for stages and things?

DR: It could be anything. Most television stations now have mobile units to do news. Lots of libraries are getting into video production. I wonder if anyone has approached you about a dual-purpose vehicle that could be used for production as well. The television people can pull vehicles up to a building, run their cords inside, and use the vehicle as a portable studio without a stage.

BM: Libraries don't have the type of equipment to get into a vehicle of that classification. Most libraries, I found, have $2,000 or $3,000 videotape machines. They have the camera and audio equipment to go with them, of course. It's possible to take the bookmobile and do it, but to my knowledge, nobody has done it.

DR: Let's get back to the mileage. It seems to me that the life and death of vehicles in the future depends on their economy.

BM: You're running into an inherited design problem when you start worrying about gas mileage on a bookmobile. Two-thirds of our heating system is derived from or delivered through free engine heat. We take the hot water from the radiator and pipe it through the floor so that it generates heat. We have been doing this for fifteen years now. Most of the heat comes from this radiant heat panel. Fuel Economy

To supplement this heat, there are electric heaters at the door entrances—a particularly cold spot in the bookmobile. When a door is opened the thermostat calls for heat. This warms the air coming in on a momentary basis, so that if the door is open for five minutes a heat current is created at the entrances. Heat is similarly provided to other places where cold air can leak in. By doing this your electric heat is not running all the time. By not putting a tremendous load on the generator, you increase its life span and consume less gasoline.

The trucks themselves are heavy. They require engines of a certain size to move them. If you try putting in a small engine to save gasoline, the dollar you save on gasoline will be spent on preventive maintenance or extra service work later on.

We go through the spec books and say, "Well, wonderful. This year they offer electronic ignition." Electronic ignition saves both fuel and maintenance. You have a choice: either go with the standard or go with the new technology. In the case of electronic ignitions, the technology has proven successful and we recommend them. We spend the dollar as wisely as possible, based on past experience.

A bookmobile conference in Maryland, the "ideal bookmobile" conference, addressed many of these questions. We found libraries that were buying a spare bookmobile because the generator never worked right. Why buy a whole new bookmobile for the sake of a generator? Why not order two generators? The way our generator works, the setup has all plug-in

type connections, so that you can change from one
generator to another in an hour. While one is out
for service, the other is in use. This eliminates
a lot of downtime. We haven't been worrying whether
the bookmobile uses ten gallons of gasoline a day
or eleven gallons because, in my mind, it is more
important to get the bookmobile out on the road
serving the people rather than using the gasoline
to drive the bookmobile into another location to
have the generator fixed.

DR: But your fuel costs may go to a dollar a gallon!

BM: We understand that a bookmobile will never
take the place of a library, but to an awful lot of
people the bookmobile is the library. How much fuel
does it take to operate your children's room in the
library? How much fuel does it take to operate your
bookmobile in the same period? I think that you will
find that fuel usage will lean heavily toward the
bookmobile.

DR: It's like Marshall McLuhan's image of a person driving full blast into the future looking into a rear view mirror. Many library administrators
are looking into the rear view mirror and all they
are seeing is a gas mileage figure. They don't compare it to what it costs to run a central library
or a children's room. If you look in the literature,
you see over and over again mobile services leading
to more branch libraries. Can you make a projection
of mobile services based on your imagination? Where
could it be in five or ten years?

BM: The bookmobile I see in the future will be
part of the library. It should be as good and as
comfortable as any library with everything in it
that a main library has but on a limited basis, because of its smaller interior. It will serve the
blind, the handicapped, the school child, and the
middle-aged. It will provide total service to the
entire population. Taxpayers will demand that they
be served. The bookmobile of the future will have a
film being screened outside while people are in the
bookmobile getting books and audiovisual materials
and having questions answered. I think the bookmobile will grow in size.

A person who enters a bookmobile is received

more warmly than a person who comes into a main library simply because it's a more personalized type
of service. You get to know the people who go on
that bookmobile. The best way to sell service is to
sell yourself to the people. The bookmobile of the
future will have to be expanded to accommodate all
these things. It's going to remain on a more or less
limited basis. But a lot of branches could be closed
and adequately operated on a bookmobile basis.

I think you will see more giant, 40-foot book
trailers, primarily because the initial investment
is relatively small and they have much more flexibility. They have a semi-permanency, so that you can
have an all-day stop. In a shopping area you can
follow the sales. If shopping area A has its sales
on Monday, shopping area B has them on Tuesday, C on
Wednesdays, you can parallel this pattern. The only
way this can happen is with an increase in purchase
of bookmobiles. The library with one bookmobile cannot possibly schedule this service; it calls for two
to five bookmobiles. We should take some of the emphasis off branch libraries and put it into mobiles,
because we have a mobile population. My own feeling
is that the bookmobile of the future will be able to
serve the total population, so that both a 16-year-
old black student and a senior citizen can get the
information they need. There has to be a more innovative use of bookmobiles. It's being done now, but
all of this has to be expanded. There are libraries,
such as the Washington County Library in Greenville,
Mississippi, that are doing it. They are doing it
today! They are doing it successfully!

DR: Do you see yourself producing modules that
could go into other mobile transports such as trains,
cars, commercial bus services, or something else of
that nature?

BM: This can be accomplished only if the libraries
follow the regionalization trend. If we had a train
run from Boston to Worcester to Springfield, I think
it would be possible. I think it's not only possible
but very practical to set up a separate train car as
a mobile library, a permanent library on a moving
route.

DR: Have you played around with this at all? Has
anybody approached you?

BM: I have had talks with several people.
I discussed this last year with a librarian
who uses the train a great deal. He thought   Trains
that it would be a wise idea to have this.
Since the businessman is financing the rail-
road, why not have a business library on each
train? Why not have a selection of paperbacks or
a selection of books in a plane? Where a train would
cross state lines, I see a New England Regional Library System, with six states involved. It's in the
realm of possibility. The guy who lives in Vermont
should have access to books in the Boston Public Library. You would need a large central collection. I
don't think that state lines should bar you from using another library. Maybe fifty years from now I see
a national library tag. If I happen to be in Louisiana on a business trip, I can go into the local public library to do some research, borrow some equipment or take out a good book. Three days later I can
walk into the San Francisco Public Library and return
that book and it will go back to Louisiana. It's a
matter of congressional responsibility. These things
cost money. I think that libraries have to do a
whole lot more in the legislative aspect. They have
to do a whole lot more politicking than they do now.

Ed Chenevert

"There is a Cerebral Palsy school where we go
once a week. Our bookmobile was designed with extrawide doors so that someone with crutches can get into it more easily. The rear door has a little hydraulic lift that has been very successful."

Ed Chenevert is the director of the Portland
(Maine) Public Library and an advocate of outreach
via media vehicles to serve retirement homes, the
handicapped, and many others.

EC: My bookmobile started out to be
a unique operation. It was designed to
serve handicapped and disadvantaged   Service
people. It was originally conceived   to the
as a Model Cities operation, except   Handicapped
that we didn't get our funding through
Model Cities. In the midst of all the
Model Cities activities in Portland, some
public housing developments were built on the city's

periphery. The bookmobile now goes all over. Its
original goal of serving the handicapped and the
disadvantaged remains. It still goes to some of the
earlier Model Cities neighborhoods, but it also
serves the disadvantaged. When there's a public
housing development in the outskirts, with a lot of
the people who used to be in the Model Cities area,
the bookmobile goes there. We are holding to our
original service goal as much as possible.

As far as the handicapped go, it's been highly
successful. One of the key places we wanted to serve
was the Cerebral Palsy Center, where kids are in
wheelchairs and stretchers. There is a Cerebral
Palsy school where we go once a week. Our bookmobile
was designed with extrawide doors so that someone
with crutches can get into it more easily. The rear
door has a little hydraulic lift that has been very
successful. We are still serving the Cerebral Palsy
Center every week.

We put on a stereo to broadcast music and activity inside. We can also broadcast outdoors through
built-in loudspeakers. I also built in a microphone
so that we could go into a neighborhood and address
a group of children: "Okay, we're going to have a
movie, or a puppet show, now." We built a screen
for movies on the side of the vehicle. It's like a
trap door—a square opens up on the outside of the
vehicle like a shadow box; on the inside we have a
rear view projector. The idea was to have the kids
sit outdoors; we would show movies through the
screen. But the rear projection screen and shadow
box did not perform as we hoped. Often there was too
much light to allow for a sharp image and shelves of
books had to be removed each time we used the screen.
When we go to a public housing development now, we
take the projector and a regular portable screen in-
doors and show a film in the community room or housing development while other people are on the bookmobile looking at books. At some quiet stops we
still show films on board using the portable screen
inside the bookmobile. I saw it as a multimedia
thing. I even built in some cubicles that can be set
up so that a kid can sit on a chair and use film
loops and filmstrips. The filmstrips have been popular. We use a Singer Auto-vance which is used on a
drop-down cubicle.

During the summer we cooperate with the parks

and recreation department and with some of the
school locations. We will bring a special program
over to accompany the bookmobile. We can bring a
puppet show or a story hour or a film program in
addition to our daily bookmobile operation.

The bookmobile has been a pilot to
test different services. For example,
we have a city hospital that is really   Reaching
a medical live-in facility for older   Shut-Ins
disadvantaged people. We started to go
over there with the bookmobile but
found that we were better off with a
little library van. Instead we put in a deposit
collection there. The librarians bring boxes of
books and a book cart and go through the wards or
the rooms of the city hospital room by room, rather
than have the bookmobile sitting outside waiting
for the patients. The same is done with some of the
senior citizen housing units. We have a lot of
apartment homes for the elderly. We started with a
bookmobile but then found that it was better to
take a van, leave a deposit collection there, or
show a film. We now use the van and can reach a lot
of shut-ins.

DR: What things would you change?

EC: I'd have the movie screen on the inside back
of the vehicle. If you want to have a program, kids
could just sit on the floor or on folding chairs
throughout the whole vehicle. There isn't too much
else I would change. The candy-striped awning is a
sexy touch, but has proved difficult to put up and
take down. It cannot be used in the rain because
water fills it up and causes it to sag.

DR: What about the software in the vehicle? Do
you check out things other than books?

EC: No longer. We have talking books. We have a
demonstration machine and a few records, but it's
not a loaning facility for talking books. I have
one professional and two paraprofessionals who are
college graduates. The staff changes. When we
started the bookmobile, it was "way-out"; we hardly
kept circulation records. When we realized that we
had to have records, had to control things, it became more traditional. We don't charge fines yet.

We charge fines throughout the rest of the library
system but we still don't charge fines on the bookmobile. We now register patrons the same way as the
rest of the library system, and the loan period is
three weeks. If you have been a delinquent borrower,
then you either can't have any more loans until you
bring the other books back, or you can only have one
or two. We try to control this problem by limiting
what we lend. If you are a new borrower with fairly
poor identification, you may be only allowed to take
one book until we have a chance, at the main library,
to check out your address and references. We discon-
tinued lending phono records due to a high loss
rate--we were loaning 100 and getting only 10 back.

DR: When you were designing this vehicle did you
work closely with Maroney to get what you wanted?

EC: I told Maroney what I wanted. They listened.
Some of the design features, like the shelving, I
would change if I were going to have the screen on
the side. I wouldn't have the screen on the side
again. I might have a portable, self-contained projection system that could be utilized outside the
bookmobile, instead of trying to project from the
vehicle itself.

DR: Were there any models that you used for this
vehicle, or was it pretty much your own concept?

EC: It was my own concept. I had thought or
dreamed of it being like a neighborhood information
center. When I was designing it, Model Cities was
in its heyday and had all kinds of "info" on places
to go for welfare, health services, and you name it.
I saw the bookmobile as a traveling information center, but it never really became that. I had hoped
we would have lots of pamphlets and give-away materials about city services or private services. The
give-away materials were taken by children and immediately turned into trash. This failure has been
disappointing.

DR: You let the service go its own way, then. You
don't try to impose direction on it yourself?

EC: I find sharp people and let them "paddle their
own canoe." Every so often I think something is off
the track and I try to get it back on. I'm trying
to give you an honest evaluation. One of my goals

was providing community and social services information. Although we do some,
this never really materialized. In the   Adult
library we have an Adult Independent   Independent
Learning Project that is tied in with   Learning
nine libraries nationally. Independent   Project
learning and the bookmobile have worked
with some people. We got their names
and got them to come into the main library to get further help. But I can't honestly say
it's a traveling adult independent learning center.
Actually, most people come into the library, sit
down with a learner's advisor, and then undertake
a learning project.

DR: What else, Ed?

EC: Preventive maintenance. The bookmobile uses
13.5 gallons of gas a week for the generator in the
winter. It has two gas tanks: one for the generator
and one for the vehicle. The generator is all-impor-
tant, so we have scrupulous preventive maintenance
and regular servicing. I think that preventive maintenance is very important. We have a good two-way
radio; it is terrific. The main receiver is in the
library. If the bookmobile wants something, if someone's sick, if we want to talk to someone on the
bookmobile, we can. It is a good radio—it comes
over better than a telephone—and we spent a little
over a thousand bucks for it. We had an awful hassle
to get the wavelength cleared.

If we could do it again, we would have the running lights connected to both the engine's system
and the auxiliary generator so that they could be
left on during night stops. We would forego air
conditioning in favor of more natural light from the
ceiling. And the doors would be better sealed to
prevent dust from getting inside and from jamming
the hydraulic wheelchair lift.

Roger Christian

"When you are sitting in a shopping center,
flashing lights attract attention. . . . We play records or the radio on outside speakers to attract
people. Use sight and sound."

Roger Christian was the director of the Washington County Library in Greenville, Mississippi, when this study was conducted.

DR: How does your mobile service go beyond the traditional bookmobile service?

RC: When I go to state and national conferences, I hear people saying the same old things: "Let's go to the people. Let's get out among the people and provide them with library service." I don't think that a stationary library can do this. As America has gone on wheels, we have to go on wheels. We have to get books out to people. Most library employees fall into the middle-income bracket and have developed the same social values and attitudes as this group. We think that just because we have a second car and can go to the library, other people can do the same anytime they want to. We think because we're interested in books, everyone else is interested in books. This is just not true. We have to get out of the library, interest people in books, libraries, and what is in them. Many people are afraid of libraries because what little contact they have had with a public library has been very negative, like the receipt of overdue notices. So we have to go to the people and one way to do this is by the mobile library. We must have as much on a mobile library as we have in the public library and offer as many services. For instance, most bookmobiles cannot provide reference service. But if you place a radio-telephone on a bookmobile—as we have done in ours—you can do this. You have to offer a card catalog or a catalog of the whole library system. We have a microfiche copy of our card catalog on the bookmobile. People's time is sought by other media: by picture shows and all the other activities in a community. There is a great demand on individuals for their time. The library has to compete for this time.

DR: Have you done any cost analysis of this in terms of how running mobile services compares to running branch libraries?

RC: The two bookmobiles circulate as many books as four of the six branch libraries in our system.

DR: I have heard figures recently that there are some libraries in this country that are circulating books to only 40 percent of the people that come through the doors. The number of people who are coming in to check out books is dropping off.

RC: I am doing a report on a survey we did. Most library surveys are taken within the library, but we mailed ours out. We have a group called Friends of the Library, and we have what we call Influence Centers. We had the president of the Friends of the Library compile a list of 100 people that she thought had the greatest influence on people in the community. We surveyed these people. Then we surveyed the high school students. So we sent our questionnaire to four different groups. Fifty-five percent of the Friends of the Library came in for reference books. Thirty-six percent of our adult patrons came for reference books. Different types of people make different use of the library. Sixty-one percent of the Influence Centers used reference books. These are used by people who are highly articulate members of the community. And 77 percent of the high school students came to the library to use reference books.

DR: Your survey results indicate that you can no longer justify running an operation on the basis of circulation statistics alone. There are certainly other ways to justify bookmobile service.

RC: You know the old cliche, "How can you justify the value of one question answered or one book per patron?" The world could turn on one bit of information and your community could be improved by the answer to one question. I don't try to justify through circulation.

DR: Is your mobile telephone used to hook people up to other community information sources as well?

RC: It could be. You can dial anyone in town or in the nation.

DR: You were more involved with the builder in the design stage than the bookmobile librarian.

RC: Yes.

DR: Does the article about your vehicle in the Mississippi Library News cover the design problems and what you would do differently if you were to design it again today?

RC: The article does mention some things that we would change.

DR: Suppose you were to start over again to build the ideal media machine. What would you do?

RC: Approach the problem from the perspective of needs. Determine what you need and what the biggest unit will do for you, instead of trying to figure out how much money you have. The more books, materials, and services you send into the community, the greater is the utility of the unit. We bought the largest bookmobile based upon that logic.

Needs before Costs

DR: Not what you could afford?

RC: No. We decided on what we needed and then tried to obtain the money, instead of vice versa. We operate our system objectively. We determine our needs and then we approach the funding agencies.

DR: What percentage of vehicle space did you sacrifice to have media playback on the machine?

RC: Most bookmobiles are designed with a person or two at the front and one at the back to see that no one takes anything off the bookmobile. We decided that we didn't need that person in the back. So we built a room there.

DR: Did that work for indoor and outdoor projection?

RC: It worked for outdoor. The rear of the bookmobile was walled off to make a 4 x 8-foot multipurpose room. The room contains small storage cabinets, a shelf, and a table for audio-visual equipment. A rear view daylight screen was built at the side of this room so that a picture could be projected on the outside wall of the unit. The sound systems center is also there; it includes a turntable, a cassette player, and an AM/FM radio. A separate eight-track player is connected to the stereo speakers on the inside of the unit. The sound system also includes outside speakers that are connected to this equipment and a microphone in the front of the unit. A 16mm projector with high intensity lamps and a

Multipurpose Room

rear view lens can project films from this multipurpose room onto the screen. The screen on the
side of the bookmobile is in this room.

DR: But it projects to the outside not inside?

RC: It projects from the inside of the room onto
the back of the screen which is viewed outside.

DR: How successful has that been?

RC: It's very good. We had trouble finding the
correct type of screen. The initial screen was not
adequate for our purpose but the Maroney Company
stayed with us and found the kind of screen that
we have now. We use it in our summer reading program. We have films each week at our libraries.
This bookmobile goes to one of our libraries that
is so small that it doesn't have a projector or
screen.

DR: What about production off the vehicles? Have
you thought in the future of doing video or anything off the vehicles?

RC: I have already. We just received other reve-
nue sharing funds: $120,000 from the county and
$80,000 from the city of Greenville. Thirty-five
thousand dollars have already been earmarked for
the purchase of another bookmobile that will serve
the city of Greenville. We had to determine the
largest size unit we could use on the roads in the
community served by the bookmobile. We decided this
time that we're going to go for the largest unit we
can buy that will work on the streets. In other
words, the size of the unit will be determined by
the physical environment, the streets of the city.
I want a video cassette player on the unit and a
TV monitor. I've already been thinking of the best
way to set these up. I thought about placing the
cassette player on a shelf that swings out from the
inside of the bookmobile.

DR: Are you talking about recording or playback
only?

RC: We record inside our library already. I
wouldn't use it for recording on the unit.

DR: The reason for the question is that there are
some people who are thinking of having modular units

that can be partially stripped and used for production. Shelves could be removed and space could be used as little studios to do community events.

RC: Okay, that might be very interesting, but we're not going to do production. I think that that requires production people.

DR: So you wouldn't compromise?

RC: No, I wouldn't compromise the use of the bookmobile. If I wanted a first class video unit, I would have a first class video unit. If I want a first class bookmobile, I want a first class bookmobile! Trying to marry the two would produce a second class system. One would take from the other. Bookmobiles must maintain strict schedules to be effective.

DR: When you talked to Maroney about a vehicle, how much did they say about economy? Was it just assumed that if you're going to have so much weight and power, you're going to spend so much per mile on gas? Did they talk about economy to you, and if so, how?

RC: We discussed it. I don't remember now the exact conversation but that was a consideration.

DR: With gasoline prices as high as they are, it seems to me that the whole future of mobile service is jeopardized by the economy. When you talk with a lot of people, they just assume continuance of present power-to-weight ratios.

RC: An article came across my desk today that says that one of the things that is in competition with bookmobiles is "books-by-mail." I also received something today saying that book rates and postal rates are going up. So if you look at everything on the whole, you conclude that it's all relative; costs for everything are increasing.

DR: When you look through bookmobile literature, nothing has been written on the subject of vehicle economy.

RC: But there was a study done. It compared mail libraries to bookmobiles.

DR: I'm talking about whether you have electronic ignition or whether you don't, whether you have fuel injection or whether you don't—the difference between just plain power and weight.

RC: The most important thing we consid-
ered was the safety of the patrons and
the staff members. We made sure that the   Safety
bookmobile met all of the safety standards
for the brakes, the emergency system, the
lighting, and the signs. We considered
everything—both economy and safety.

DR: People I've talked to who have gone through
the whole process are told: "There's a certain power,
a certain weight, and that's it!" They are never
told about electronic ignitions or fuel injection,
or anything else. They are not told specifically
what that company is doing about fuel savings.

RC: At the time that we bought this unit,
from the time of purchase until we let the
contract, there was nothing on the horizon   Fuel
concerning fuel costs or fuel shortages.   Costs
That was not a priority with us at the
time. We weren't as conscious as people
are today of fuel costs.

DR: When I started to talk to Bob Maroney about it,
he said they did have discussions with International
Harvester about electronic ignitions, but at first
he didn't understand the question either.

RC: I think that you have a valid point there. I
wasn't as conscious of fuel economy as I should have
been. I was looking for safety and service to the
people. I was looking at economy but not fuel economy
as such. I wanted to find the best heavy-duty equipment that would carry the books. The library board
did discuss fuel cost and was concerned. But I don't
remember how the discussion went or what we determined concerning fuel cost.

DR: Auxiliary power: that's one of the big pains in
the neck. Have you had difficulty there?

RC: I think that the secret with auxiliary power is
to have a good service organization. We found that
our local distributor had neither the equipment nor
the knowledge to cope with our unit. This is where
Bob Maroney and his company stood with us. We called
and told them the problem we were having and he suggested that we take the unit to Little Rock, Arkansas,
to a distributor of the Kohler Company there. I went
two times. The first time I drove the unit over. They

didn't get the job done. I drove it over a second time and they worked on it all day. That's been a year and a half or more ago. It's never been back. The secret is to have a good service organization or a good company to work with. Second is preventive maintenance. Your driver must be conscious of that unit and must take care of it. If you do those two things, if you take care of the equipment, follow procedures, follow the directions on the maintenance brochures, and have a good service organization or a good manufacturer's representative, that takes care of most of the problem.

DR: Did you start with a new staff on your new vehicle or did they move off an old vehicle? If so, how did that transition work?

RC: We planned the unit here. I ordered the unit even before a librarian came on board. When the new librarian came in, she went on the bookmobile. There was no transition period. But the staff that we have now on an old unit (it's a 1952 or 1955 model Gerstenslager) is looking forward to going to whatever new unit is chosen. We are not to the stage where we have selected a new unit. We don't know yet if it will be a Gerstenslager or a Maroney or some other type of unit manufactured by another company. But the staff is looking forward to going on the new bookmobile.

We find very good acceptance from the majority of our staff. We have high speed tape duplicators on board; a video cassette player/recorder; a sound system and cordless headsets in the library—just about every type of modern equipment. Audiovisual circulation has jumped from 3,800 in 1973-74 to 5,500 in 1974-75. It's almost doubled on the AV equipment. There is no staff resistance.

DR: What other things would you like to say to potential mediamobile builders?

RC: I would not place a screen in the rear of the unit. We discussed video cassettes and 16mm film. If you place the screen in the rear of the unit and you have to use your auxiliary power, there is competition between generator noise and the film sound. If you can run an extension

Better
Equipment
Location

from a pole off a building, you don't have that problem. In this new unit, if we can go with the TV, we
will place it toward the front. We will also place
the equipment on the floor of the unit so we do not
have to cart a set on a stand. We decided that it
would be better if we placed the 16mm projector on
the floor. Usually we have to pick it up and place
it on a table and then set it back down after the
movie is over. Have the equipment located where it
will not have to be moved. And do not have it at the
rear of the vehicle.

DR: How much looking at other vehicles did you do?

RC: We did quite a bit. We went to Little Rock,
Arkansas. I went to other libraries, but the board
members went to Little Rock.

DR: What's in Little Rock?

RC: Little Rock has a large Gerstenslager.

DR: Is that a media integrated vehicle?

RC: No. They do not have what we have on this one.

DR: What did you look at in the way of integrated
vehicles?

RC: We didn't look at any integrated vehicles. We
thought we were the first ones. I couldn't find any
literature at the time concerning the things that I
wanted on it. We didn't have any point of reference
with other units concerning the use of nonprint materials.

DR: When was your unit built?

RC: It took us nine or ten months from the time we
ordered the bookmobile and we've had it about two
years. May 2, 1973, was the date it was submitted for
bid. The unit was delivered on January 17, 1974.

DR: I think that when you ordered your unit the
Berkeley one had been running for three, maybe four,
years.

RC: We didn't know about it at the time.

DR: Any other things, Roger?

RC: We like the seats that turn because they are
multipurpose. The driver and the assistant librarian
sit at the front and can reverse themselves for a

patron. They have desks built behind them. They sit behind the desk when they get to their stop. We have a light system on top of the bookmobile that flashes—small lights like those used on emergency vehicles. I envisioned a much larger light. You have to watch the law, though, to determine what color you can use in your own particular state. I use flashing amber lights.

DR: It must be an attention-getter.

RC: That's right. When you are sitting in a shopping center, flashing lights attract attention. They are very success- **Attracting** ful in Little Rock, but ours here has not **Attention** been as successful at shopping centers as I had hoped. You can get lost in a shopping center regardless of the size of the unit. If you get a rotating light, you do attract people. We play records or the radio on outside speakers to attract people. Use sight and sound.

I would not have paperback racks in the aisle. We had to take them off because the vibration of the unit from the stopping and starting caused the paperback racks to break. I would not use a rotary paperback rack. Fortunately, Maroney had the foresight to leave the cutouts from our carpet.

DR: Can't the racks be strengthened with welding?

RC: They probably could, but we felt that it took up too much space in the center of the vehicle. We decided to place the paperbacks at the front, near the librarian.

WESTON WOODS

Morton Schindel

"A mediamobile is designed to house people. It is a place of public assembly. It is a place where the whole program is delivered along with, and by, the facilities of the vehicle. This means that it has to be air conditioned and heated. It requires much more power than a bookmobile."

Morton Schindel is the president and director

of Weston Woods—one of the pioneers in the design
and marketing of media vehicles.

   MS: We got into mediamobiles because we were making films for children. We felt that communities
have, through private financing, built specialized
cinemas for adults and they haven't done it for children. We also create a multimedia mixer program of
adaptations of children's books. This is how we got
into the multimediamobile.

   Some years ago we had an order from a school system for a print of everything that we had made. It
was interesting enough, because we already had had
a good many orders from the school system. I called
the head of audiovisuals and I said, "From the looks
of this order, you have something special. What are
you doing?" He said, "We want to see if we can in-
duce reluctant readers to read by exposing them to
all kinds of audiovisual materials related to these
books. We know that when a book is adapted for the
theater, the paperback editions come out and they
sell millions of books." So I said, "That's great
and we are happy to participate."

   About a year went by and I was invited by a college in that same area to be a guest lecturer in one
of their children's literature courses. I went largely because it would give me an opportunity to survey
what the people in that area had done with this program. The college representatives said that the board
of education had a great idea; they received funding
from Washington and called together some of the key
people in school libraries in that particular dis-
trict--from about 40 schools in all. These key people
took all of the information, went back to their district, and got in touch with the principals of the
40 schools. The principals also thought it was a
fine idea and approved of their school librarians'
participation. The school librarians were interested;
they in turn told teachers in their respective ele-
mentary schools, so the information finally got down
from the board of education to the teachers.

   The materials had to get out. The librarians had
one print each of a number of films to circulate
around the 40 schools. A film was not always in the
school when it was expected to be there. Even if it
was in the school when it was scheduled, the equipment didn't always work. And even if the equipment
was in operable condition, you could not necessarily

darken the room nor could you always find someone
to operate the machine. Therefore, once the good
idea of the board of education had filtered down to
the youngsters, the impact was so watered down that
it was as if there were no program at all.

Our first vehicles were actually
adapted school buses. We used old
school buses that were no longer good   Adapted
enough to transport children, but were   School
good enough to house them. Some of   Buses
these vehicles are still on the road
after ten years and they deliver the
same program with the same effective-
ness as the new ones. We thought it
would be very exciting for vocational high schools
to undertake projects like this with their super-
annuated school buses. Not only would they be creating a facility but working on something like this,
repairing a ten-year-old, four-door sedan, has such
motivational value that, inevitably, some of the
graduates of that school are going to want to work
as technicians on that vehicle themselves. So you
can see how that could be self-generating. This is
the type of activity we would like to help.

In the final analysis, we have discovered that
the key to successful use of a facility of this sort
is a dedicated staff and an administration that is
innovative in its thinking. This does require strong
administrative support right from the top of the
institution. We have found that the various programs
that we've been involved with since 1966 were just
as good as the people. Good people, somehow or other,
care about the vehicle, keep it running. This gets
into the audiences that come aboard it. It's a re-
warding activity.

DR: How did you get started on the Children's
Caravan project?

MS: Originally the idea grew out of the need to
find a vehicle to use as the format for a children's
television show. If a bookmobile was the most exciting context in which children came together with
books, a mediamobile would be an exciting context
for children to come together with films that were
designed for them. Our first Showmobile, Children's
Caravan, was built in 1963. I think it was the first
vehicle of its kind put together and intended as a

film showing device. It had a rolling sea of red
carpet built into it. There were rounded steps that
the children would sit on. It had a great aisle down
the middle like the school bus—the model from which
it was originally derived.

DR: Where did you take it from there?

MS: We were approached by the Office of Economic
Opportunity to create a number of these vehicles for
use in Appalachia and in the rural South. The librarians and teachers who were using them reported back
to us that the built-in seats were limiting the use
of space. Working from the experience they had derived operating six of them over a period of several
years, we began to develop the present mediamobile.

The difference, incidentally, between a mediamobile and a bookmobile, as I see it, is this: A bookmobile is an attractive means of taking books out of
the library to where the people are. Essentially, it
is a delivery vehicle. People do not sit in a bookmobile and read their books; they come in and get them,
check them out, take them home, and the next time
the bookmobile comes back, they bring them back and
get some more. It's almost like any other vending
service that is mobile.

On the other hand, a mediamobile is designed to
house people. It is a place of public assembly. It
is a place where the whole program is delivered
along with, and by, the facilities of the vehicle.
This means that it has to be air conditioned and
heated. It requires much more power than a bookmobile because projectors draw current, as do heaters
and air conditioners.

There is a close correlation between the effec-
tiveness of communication and the context in which
that communication takes place. For example, there's
no better way to communicate a story to a youngster
than to place him on a soft couch, in front of a
fire, with nice lighting. This creates an emotional
tone for the story that the parent is going to read.
Put that same child in a big classroom with 40 or
50 other kids, get the teacher in front with a little book like "Peter Rabbit" that the youngster
can't see, because the teacher is looking at the
pages, and you can see that it is hardly a context
for communication to compare with a loving mother's
knee.

Now we get into mediamobiles. The lighting of
the vehicle, the decoration, all these elements are
developed to create a predisposition to the program.
For example, if the program on a mediamobile were
going to be science, I think it would follow that
the design of the vehicle—the decor, if you will—
might be quite different. This decor might be created by things that are hung on the walls or something of that sort. I would think of light blues and
chromium for example, rather than the warmer hues of
a red carpet and a gold curtain.

DR: Let's consider the integration of technology
into the vehicle. You have discussed the environmental aspect. I would like to hear how the integration
of electronics into a vehicle works, how you've approached this.

MS: First of all, suppose we talk about
lighting. The lighting on a vehicle of
this sort gives adequate room on walls.   Lighting
It's like theater lighting. It can dim so
that when the image comes on the screen,
we can create a comfortable transition
from the world of reality to the world
of illusion on the screen. The screen
area on the mediamobile is a rear view screen that
can be removed so that same area can be used as a
puppet stage. These vehicles need to be designed so
that there are outlets for hanging light spots or
whatever for participation or dramatic presentation.
Obviously, at the same time, we have all types of
safety lights for exits. We must have a light to go
on in case of a power failure; this is activated or
powered by a battery. The lighting has to be developed so that the vehicle can be segmented. That way
more than one program can be comfortably conducted
at the same time. You would do this by having dim
lights or no lights in the front while you are showing a film to one group of youngsters, while in the
rear, separated by a black curtain with another
teacher or librarian, another group selects books
to take home.
        Inevitably when you have air conditioners on,
when there is a generator running, you have a level
of sound that you have to cope with. With a good
public address system, you could adjust speakers in
the front, back, and outside of the vehicle at dif-

ferent levels. All of these features should be built
into the walls of the vehicle.

DR: What about the generator?   **2116670**

MS: The cable must be designed so that when it is
connected to the local power, the electrical current
is not on. The flow of current must be a second oper-
ation--or the electrical system would blow up. There
must be absolute safety controls to insure that these
things are properly handled.

Let's now consider the visual elements. There
are two ways to do this: one is rear screen, the
other is to project from the front. There is a third
way, individualization, that would be for small
viewing groups or individuals. We have discovered
that the rear screen is, by far, superior. The theater space or interior of the vehicle does not have
to be entirely darkened. You can't have youngsters
stick their fingers up and interfere with the presentation. It keeps them away from the projector. It
keeps the sound of the projector out of the theater.
It has flexibility; the screen can be removed,
folded up, and put away. When you remove that screen
on the vehicle that we make, another screen can be
pulled into place like a double hung window. You
have a front screen if you need it. There are tables
and plugs along the walls if you want to have a number of youngsters exposed to different audiovisual
presentations.

DR: I'm also interested in the television and tele-
communication aspects, and how they affect reference
work.

MS: We have installed both in these vehicles for
various clients. There are many people who are not
aware that the reference section is there in Buffalo,
New York. The Buffalo/Erie County Library has one of
these. They wanted to install a telephone so that
they could demonstrate this access system to the public. In Bedford/Stuyvesant they had another telephone
installed for safety purposes. They are working in
an area where they would feel remiss in their obliga-
tion to the staff if they didn't have one aboard for
emergency purposes. We all have to be prepared for
further developments in the age of television. One

would want to transmit television programs using the vehicle as a context. These might be open circuit programs. They might be coming off video cassettes. Both of these are possible with the installation of a relatively simple antenna on the outside; we have done both.

DR: You sell the vehicle and you are thinking about leasing the vehicles. I wonder if you could discuss these arrangements?

MS: We are very conservative people by nature. We wanted to be absolutely sure when we delivered any quantity of these vehicles that the problems and bugs were worked out. We entered into an arrangement with two libraries in different parts of the country where the climatic problems were different and also where the intended range of programming would be different. We participated in the financing of these vehicles, which is simply a nice way of saying that we only asked the buyers to pay a portion of the cost of building them, with the understanding that together we were debugging by developing these mediamobiles. All of us felt that we should: this was something that was being done in the interest of the profession as well as the libraries' own programs.

Both of these vehicles have been on the road for about one year. They have been helpful to us in both of these locations. We learned about refinements that are now being put into not only their vehicles, at our expense, but also into all of the new ones we are creating. When you buy an automobile, you have one place where you take it for service—to the dealer where you bought it. If you buy a school bus or a bookmobile, practically everything is serviced in one place by one organization. A mediamobile has a variety of equipment. It has a generator that is purchased from, and serviced by, someone other than the chassis and body manufacturer. It has audiovisual equipment that is purchased from, and serviced by, a completely different organization. It has air conditioners. We wanted to explore how effectively a piece of sophisticated equipment like this could be maintained.

Maintenance

We have leased a vehicle to a school system. This is a vehicle that we garage, maintain, and insure.

It's our job to see that it's ready to
be picked up by the school's drivers
every morning and that when it goes out   Leasing
it is clean and that everything is op-
erable. We, of course, are paid for
that service. It's our initial reaction
that this is a more satisfactory system
from the point of view of the person
who is going to use it. And if it's more satisfactory from their point of view, it's more satisfactory from our point of view, because continuous and
effective use is our concern. This is not a new idea.
I believe there are many libraries or big systems
today that rent things like International Business
Machines (IBM) computers. IBM rents computers to insure that they are properly maintained and always
ready for effective use. We think there may be some
parallel in the way we could most effectively make
a service like this available.

There's one other possibility that we will be
exploring before the end of the year. We're thinking
of actually operating the vehicles ourselves, rendering service in accordance with the programs outlined
by a community. We would, in effect, hire the librarians or the presenters and work out the program with
people in the community. The reason for this is that
this vehicle requires specialized expertise in its
operation. One person normally drives, maintains,
and operates all the equipment. The second person,
in effect, is the presenter of the program. This also requires a specialized kind of training. Our en-
gaging, training, and supervising a corps of people
of that sort would wind up rendering a better service than if the activity is administered locally
by each institution that needs the service.

Bill Miles

"People don't put enough time into considering
the kind of environment they will have inside a vehicle and the kind of flexibility they should build
into it. Your interior should be a modular type of
structure so that you can rearrange it. At times
you may want to change your whole interior around—
readapt it and vary the kinds of things that you do."

Bill Miles is a deputy director at the Buffalo/
Erie County Library in Buffalo, New York. He has

used mobile service imaginatively in serving target groups in the inner city and on Indian reservations.   .

DR: What would you do differently now? What problems have you had to correct? What would you advise people to avoid?

BM: I would be concerned with the size of the generator. When we bought the RAM (Readily Accessible Materials) Van unit, it was using 750kw. The power was not sufficient for the load that was being put on it. If we used the air conditioners in the summertime and were showing a videotape and had the lights on, the generator overloaded. While it was new it ran, but it was running at peak capacity. A year ago I changed the generator from a 750kw to a 1200kw. That will run just about anything in sight. My advice is to have a generator with a margin of capacity built into it to reduce maintenance costs. When a generator is operating at peak, it burns up quickly. Have a generator with enough capacity so that if you expand your hardware and you start using more equipment, it will not be overloaded.

I would also be concerned with the kind of interior that you put into a vehicle, depending on location. When I say interior, I mean the whole environment on the inside. People don't put enough time into considering the kind of environment they will have inside a vehicle and the kind of flexibility they should build into it. Your interior should be a modular type of structure so that you can rearrange it. At times you may want to change your whole interior around—readapt it and vary the kinds of things that you do. If your sections are all the same size across, you can change them from the front to the back or the back to the front.

Modular
Interior

Be sure that you have the proper chassis. If you are going to have a conventional chassis, then buy one that will be structurally capable of handling what you have on the vehicle now and what you may want to put on it later. If you want to convert the inside into a mobile studio and you have the wrong kind of chassis under it, you will have structural problems. I'm just mentioning this to be sure

that people don't cheat themselves on what they're
buying. They might be saving money today, but the
chassis will cost them a bundle a year or two later
if they want to change something that they hadn't
anticipated. Don't forget power steering problems.
You have to be very careful to plan what you're
putting into the vehicle so it can do what you want
it to do.

DR: You're running both bookmobiles and mediama-
chines. What's your feeling about integrating these
machines?

BM: All of our trucks have charge out machines on
them. The small ones are modeled on the "Lookie
Bookie II," the other media van that we have.
"Lookie Bookie" circulates books—it's moving more
books than anything else. It's only a fraction of
the size of the tractor trailers but, on a compara-
ble basis, it's doing as much circulation as they
are. It also has the capacity to show rear view projection and street corner type stuff. It's smaller
but it can be turned into a dynamite circulation
outfit. For us here in Buffalo during the cold
months, that's primarily what it does, because nobody is going to sit down on the street corner and
look at movies. But it will hold eight or ten people to show movies on the inside tube. It's a
Chevrolet delivery van, primarily a circulation
unit that has the same features on it that the RAM
Van does. It has its own heat and air conditioning,
its own eight track cassette tape deck and an AM/FM
radio. It has the same charge out equipment that our
bookmobile uses. It goes to smaller places that
don't generate the volume of circulation that justify a larger unit, as well as places that bigger
units can't readily service.
    The unit that I put together in the future will
be a combination of the RAM Van and a tractor trailer, but it will probably have a transit-type chassis. It will be designed to circulate books. When
we do another one it will probably be a bookmobile
concept with the kind of thing that they are doing
in Missouri. There's something like it down in
Houston. They were made after the RAM Van was made
and they both have a lot of things incorporated into them like our RAM Van. The one in Missouri is
more of a bookmobile, in that it carries more books

than the RAM Van does, but the basic concept is the
same. The one in Houston is nearly the same as the
one here. When the RAM Van was being constructed, I
believe that Mary Tom Reid was up in Connecticut and
she incorporated a lot of the ideas on it.

DR: Have you been able to work out the telecommu-
nication problems? How did you come to grips with
the telephone company?

BM: I'm using two-way radio on a government frequency. I don't have radios on all of my units because I don't have the money. I can communicate with
the RAM Van at any place and it can call me.

DR: Did you have to go through the Federal Communications Commission (FCC) to get this?

BM: The FCC had already allocated this frequency
to our county government, so all I had to do was to
hook up with the county communication people. Everyone thought that it would take me a long time, so I
smiled at them and began to politic with the people
at Chessman Ridge who run the antennae up there.
Then I told the county communications director that
this was something we would like to hook into. He
was pretty understanding and let it slide through.
It's been used for the past year or so on the RAM
Van. I'm going to have all of my trucks hooked up to
it as soon as I get the money for the equipment.

DR: Is it connected in any way to your reference
services, or is it just so you can talk to your
units?

BM: No, this particular one right now
is not doing any reference. That is be-
cause the frequency is strictly for emer-   Emergency
gency use. I would put reference into an-   Mobile
other unit that wouldn't involve a high   Radio
band or low band operation that comes
under FCC regulations. It would be something that would involve the telephone company and
that is expensive. I've got some statistics on that.
I have seen some other ways of doing it—it could
even be done through a combination of a telephone
and teletype hookup that already exists.

DR: So you're planning to buy a two-way radio for
each vehicle?

BM: Yes, for emergency communication. A reference hookup would require other equipment because it isn't feasible to use high band or low band radio for it.

DR: Tell me more about the emergency radio.

BM: The system has a remote control console and a 60 watt mobile. You can buy 100 watt, 60, 45 or 30 watt mobiles. The choice depends on how far you plan to transmit. I can pick up about two or three other people on it because it is local government frequency. You have to get the kind of frequency you want to deal with. It can be high band, it can be low band; it depends on the geography and the kinds of things you want to go through it.

DR: How are you using your portapack video equipment in the van? How much video use have you had?

BM: We do at least seven programs every day just on the RAM Van. That means we see the same group at least every two weeks. To have a program it's impossible to buy enough commercial media—whether it be slides, strips, whatever. We end up using a lot of videotape doing the programs on our RAM Van because of the flexibility it allows users and because of the budget controls it allows us. After we record a tape, we can either keep it for another program or just erase it. Tapes are used quite a bit. Over the past three years we have probably used every 16mm film in our collection, so we have to have some other flexible kind of software—which usually ends up being videotape. Video is used quite extensively on our van. We keep an outline of every program so that it can be used again. The outline says what you used in it, what software you used (whether it was tape or a 16mm film), what concepts were used, and what you talked about. That's very important. You can't keep coming up with fresh ideas. When you have some people who do have ideas, imagination, and talent, you have to capitalize on it. Someday you might not have those people and you will have to revert to using past tapes.

DR: Can you tell me about energy, mobility, and whether mobile service will survive?

BM: The generators, as you know, are used when you can't plug into a place. That doesn't mean that you run your generator seven hours per day. You

plug into a source of electrical current wherever
you can. I sent out 100 letters to people across
the country on mobiles. It's amazing how many people
don't have generators, who plug into sources of existing power where they are. Whether it's at a
school, or a community center, we plug in. Our generator allows us the flexibility to serve where we
want to serve.

DR: What if the energy crisis gets to the point
where it gets too expensive to plug in?

BM: I don't think it will ever reach that point.
Maybe two out of every 100 people say that bookmobiles are in trouble because of the energy shortage.
That's a bunch of bunk. I don't thing there is a
fuel crisis. There may be an energy crisis but there
are fuel alternatives. At present, our regular fuel
is gasoline, but propane is a possibility. There are
generators that can be hooked up to a Wankel engine
that can get oodles of time on it. When you spread
out the generator time and the plug in time along
with the amount of electricity, the cost is minimal.
We make about 100 mobile stops. These are at schools;
you only see them twice a month and you only plug in
for about two or three hours. That doesn't even come
to a dollar per month. The generators run on gasoline, but the cost of the generator fuel as opposed
to a permanent library structure can be weighed in
terms of flexibility. In some places the only kind
of service that you give is through a mobile unit. I
didn't have any problem when there was a fuel shortage in Buffalo because fuel was always there. I do
see this country coming to the point where the law
won't allow anything on the road but vehicles that
get 20 miles on a gallon of gasoline. I don't see
that restriction being put on public service vehicles
like fire trucks and bookmobiles unless the economy
comes to the point where it is bottoming out so ter-
ribly that everything else is off the road anyway.

DR: I have heard stories from bookmobile people
throughout the country stating that at the end of
their line they perhaps serve 25 people, checking
out 100 books or so every two weeks. Some of these
places are getting cut out. The question is whether
mobile vehicles would have greater circulation and
invite more people to come out if the environment of
the vehicle were different.

BM: The places that do that kind of business shouldn't have a big bookmobile. This is the advantage of having various kinds and sizes of units. I can take the "Lookie Bookie," which is small and doesn't burn up all the fuel that a tractor trailer does, to the Indian reservation. There was once a bookmobile stop on the Indian reservation, and then a small library was placed in the Community Center, but it was not generating circulation because no one could be there all the time. Right now I'm servicing the reservation with the "Lookie Bookie." The library has been closed down in the Community Center so big trucks don't go there, but the "Lookie Bookie" does and generates as much use as the library did. As a matter of fact, it is generating about five times as much use as the library did over a period of a month, and we're only there a couple of hours per week. In other words, you can still provide service but it should be tailor-made service. Say for instance you have got small stops that you think are strategic enough to serve and you're only getting a circulation of 100 books out of them. Why send in a big unit when you can send in a small unit like the "Lookie Bookie" that can handle such circulation? It is custom-made for small places.

DR: How many more people would show up at the vehicle, especially on the Indian reservation, if it were "media-ized?" What do you have to do to justify that?

BM: You can bring a variety of programs. You basically do programs on this unit that you couldn't do with other bookmobiles. You can do information and entertainment programs. You can have the kind of service that can be interfaced. The justification comes in the increase in the variety of library service that you can provide with a mobile unit.

DR: Have you worked out any kind of formula for making the jump from the small book van to a vehicle that uses media to pull people in?

BM: If it's a place that's a problem and media will help stimulate the people to use library service, use media. If this doesn't work, use the people out there to do your outreach work in these locations. That's something else that's important to have, a field person who can move around through your bookmobile or through your mobile network, keeping up with what's happening the same way our inner city people used to do. You can't keep up with fragmented problems by having a bookmobile library and a "do it while they are there" atmosphere. You must have someone out there constantly selling the product and talking to people the same way you do in the city. This is one of the big things that mobile people must do: they need an outreach person oriented to mobile problems. You cannot rely on the feedback you get from people who are busy while they are there. You must have people who can do outreach as well.

Change your scheduling—that's important, too. A whole lot of people don't use the proper locations to begin with. They don't use volume locations. They don't use locations that have a built-in advantage that will help you establish your service. Many bookmobile people do two schedulings a year, one for the summer and one at the end of summer. I have a person on scheduling all year. If, during the middle of the year, a stop doesn't look like it's doing well and is not improving, a decision must be made whether to keep this place or discover another one. A lot of people hold onto stops strictly out of habit. That's bad because you end up going to places that are not doing anything for you and you're not doing anything for them, either. You must develop service planning and make minor changes all year around.

Mary Tom Reid

"[Our van] has a tremendous future. I just wish we had a fleet of 15 of them that were operational. It's one of the greatest programs I've ever seen. The main problem is keeping it on the road."

Mary Tom Reid works for the Houston Public Library. She has had experience working through problems inherent in complex, media-ized vehicles.

DR: I'd like to know what problems you've had with the vehicle and what you'd do over again if you could.

MR: One of the problems we've had was the self-contained generator. It's given us quite a bit of trouble. It was housed so that the oil had to be put in from the inside. We had red carpeting and there was a bit of trouble because of that. We should be able to add oil from the outside. Because of our climate we had to have a special air conditioning unit put in that gave us some problems.

DR: Have you beaten these problems?

MR: They are still hanging on. We are trying to beat them, but we haven't solved them at this time.

DR: What would you do differently?

MR: As far as the interior design goes, there are a lot of features I like. I like the puppet theater. I would expand it so that we would have more room in that area, so that adults would have a little more operating room behind the stage.

DR: What else?

MR: More shelving space for library materials, filmstrips, cassettes.

DR: Do you use the tables much?

MR: The tables have to be lowered when we have large groups of children for story hours. During transit, everything has to be taken down; they are not built to hold materials during traveling. This entails a lot of work for the staff. We also need more storage space for chairs, tables, and other materials.

DR: What would be your advice to someone building one of these vehicles?

MR: Give consideration to the fact that you're going to be serving large numbers of people with a lot of traffic. You need to be sure that the exits, steps, and side entrances are easy and accessible to children, including preschoolers, kindergarteners, and school-age children. Sometimes we have to be outside to help them aboard. It's very difficult for a small child to get aboard. We had to have seat belts installed after the vehicle was delivered because of the safety factors. I would also recommend a different type of reflection mirror for the rear projection screen.

DR: What's wrong with the mirror?

MR: It's just not suitable for the type of materi-

als. It's easily damaged in transit if you fail
to get a bolt tightened down properly. It can be
scratched and that mars the whole movie screen.

DR: Is the sound system adequate?

MR: The sound system is great. Terrific. You
couldn't ask for a better sound system. We added
some additional equipment so that we could have stereo inside the van. I would recommend that people
consider stereo components for the sound system, because with the records and cassettes that we are using today, you would rather use a stereo than a mon-
aural system.

DR: Anything else for the prospective builder and
operator?

MR: I think there needs to be some work done on
the flooring and the housing around the driver and
staff seats. It's not very practical to have carpeting there. At the present time there are plans to
put in linoleum or another type of flooring that can
be cleaned easily. It's not easy to keep a carpet
clean that has that much traffic. It's fine where
the children are seated for programming, but to have
it in the entrances and exits of the van is not very
practical.

DR: What about servicing the vehicle?

MR: Well, our servicing is done at the city garage.
It's out of warranty now so the city garage takes
care of it.

DR: So you don't go to the dealer for overall chassis maintenance?

MR: That's one of the problems we've had with the
van. There were several companies that were involved
in this. One company—the company that was supposedly the designer of the van—did not have a local out-
let here. That's one of the things that operators
need to check out. We had to take the body to another
company. The generator was put in by a special firm
located across the city, and the chassis was taken
care of by International. We had to have three different sources servicing the van while it was still
under warranty. This was an unusual situation because
Weston Woods delivered the shell of the van and then
tried to finish work on it here, which was not very

practical. It should have been done at their shop in Weston rather than in a city several thousand miles away. It has been very difficult to get the repairs and work done on it.

DR: What do you see as the future of this van?

MR: It has a tremendous future. I just wish we had a fleet of 15 of them that were operational. It's one of the greatest programs I've ever seen. The main problem is keeping it on the road. Of course people will say, "Well, you have to consider that with mechanical things," but I think we've had a somewhat unusual number of mechanical problems that we should have been able to cope with. For various reasons, we've felt that we couldn't get them taken care of as quickly as they should have been.

DR: Do you have any parting words for anybody who might run one of these machines?

MR: Well, just be sure that it's checked out thoroughly and in proper operation before you accept delivery on it.

DR: The article in the Texas Library Journal about your machine is a good one.

MR: Yes, I believe that our program has unlimited potential. It's the way to reach people who cannot receive service from the ordinary library. The out-reach program is something that all libraries are looking for and is a great thing for us.

GAMETIME

Julian Serrill

"We've tried our media vehicle in areas where they've had no previous bookmobile service. It's been used mostly at parks and playgrounds, making a series of scheduled stops."

Julian Serrill, a librarian at the Memphis-Shelby County Library in Tennessee, worked closely with Game-time to get the library's vehicle on the road. His practical, no nonsense approach covers the design and use of the vehicle and the later planning for another.

DR: I'm interested in what went right and what went wrong. What advice would you give to people planning a media vehicle, as opposed to a straight bookmobile?

JS: We started in June of 1972. We were happy that we did what we did. We are happy with the size of it, too. Maintenance-wise and cost-wise, media vehicles are cheaper than the large bookmobile. They appeal to children, especially.

DR: Has the staff used the vehicle as it was designed?

JS: Yes, for showing movies, using the record players, tape recorders, and so forth.

DR: If you had it to do over again, how might you do it better?

JS: We have contracted for another one that will be a couple of feet larger. We had to go through bids on that. It will not be a Gametime product, because Gerstenslager bid lower.

DR: Have you encountered any problems with the present vehicle in terms of maintenance?

JS: Maintenance-wise it has been virtually trouble-free.

DR: Do you have a preventive maintenance program?

JS: Well, we have our own maintenance man in the library who does minor work on the unit. He tries to keep up a preventive program. The air conditioner was insufficient for this climate, so on the new one we are ordering two rooftop air conditioners instead of the one that we have on our old vehicle.

DR: What software do you carry on the vehicle?

JS: Well, we have magazines, along with books—mostly paperbacks. The shelving was designed so that the paperback racks can be double-shelved.

DR: Do you circulate anything besides print?

JS: We have cassettes and records.

DR: Do you look for anything else in the way of circulation of nonprint?

JS: I would like to do more on the new machine when we get it. This one was primarily for the disadvantaged program. The new machine is replacing an old bookmobile.

DR: In your staffing of the vehicle, did you get a traditional staff to come into this changed vehicle or was it a different staff?

JS: Well, it's staff that we picked from people who wanted to work with the disadvantaged. We have a staff of three.

Staffing the Vehicle

DR: I found in talking to other people that sometimes a media-ized vehicle doesn't work because staff come on with bookmobile background—they don't know how to make the projection or the sound system work.

JS: We've tried our media vehicle in areas where they've had no previous bookmobile service. It's been used mostly at parks and playgrounds making a series of scheduled stops.

DR: I talked to Jim Benzing at Gametime and went over some design problems. Do you see any need for radio on the vehicle? He said you don't find a necessity for that.

JS: No.

DR: Are you looking for anything else in the way of communication? For example, a unit in Portland, Maine, has a two-way radio unit so it can do reference work.

JS: We might experiment with two-way radio on one of our bookmobiles. I don't know which one. We have just received a grant for information referral programs.

DR: But radio would be an addition and not a basic design item in the new one?

JS: Yes, that's right.

DR: In this study, I'm concerned with an integrated approach to design rather than adding things on. Is there anything else you want to tell vehicle builders?

JS: I'd like to get rid of our two big bookmobiles and go to smaller vehicles. That would be my recommendation because of the economy of operating smaller units. If you change bookmobiles into media vehicles, you have a much more attractive vehicle. You can also transport more of the materials people can find in a branch. You can do programming for people like senior citizens, for example.

DR: Have you ever had any problem with vandalism in your vehicle?

JS: No, it is parked inside. The new one will be parked outside and we are a little concerned about what might happen.

NEW YORK TELEPHONE COMPANY

John McLuckie

"[Our vehicle] has been used as a telephone company business [office] on the street where we handle bill and rate explanations, take complaints, and sell merchandise. . . . It has been in demand for health testing because people like the accessibility. It has been very good for health testing because it's got plenty of power on board to operate equipment."

John McLuckie is an engineer for the New York Telephone Company. He designed and then supervised the company's first Mobile Community Center.

JM: Let me start with what's wrong with it. The overhead cabinets have been a failure because people are too short for them and the weight is placed too high. On the new one, I'm going for bin storage under the seats. I'm also going for more display shelves in the new one. The old one has a long display shelf but there is only one level and there is no room, because of the cabinets, to put an eye-level shelf between. In the new one I'm not putting up any cabinets. I have a long, L-shaped settee that goes down one side, then makes a right angle turn up behind the driver. The entire area underneath that is simply bin storage. Since everything falls down when you're driving, you might as well put it in divided bins so that it doesn't slide around.

The only exception to that will be things like 35mm and 16mm projectors, that will be stored in cabinets where they can't flop around. The new one will

have a 10-inch wide shelf behind the settee that also goes around this long L. It's about 12 feet long.
Above it, halfway up the wall, will be another shelf
for display purposes.

The width and length of the vehicle have not
been a problem. It looks and feels enormous, but fortunately it's easy to handle. The old unit was too
high and we had troubles going under bridges. The
new one is about 18 inches lower. That loses us a
lot of head room inside and we have to offset the
air conditioner forward. We also have to offset the
lighting to one side so that the people don't go
parting their scalps on it. There is no real need
for a desk per se. The desk has rarely been used as
a desk. I have used standard recreational vehicle
equipment. We're putting fixtures in the floor where
we can plug in removable 18-inch square tables. We
will be able to plug these into a floor fixture that
will give us the capability of having a desk for eye-
ball-to-eyeball conversations.

Gas heat has been a problem. New York's fire
laws forbid the filling and recharging of propane
tanks. We also cannot take a tank through a tunnel
and must always use the George Washington Bridge. In
the new vehicle we will use a water-cooled, detuned
Opel engine generator set, that will put out about
8500 watts. We will recover the heat from that engine to heat the body so there will be no furnace.
There will be a separate air conditioner—a bigger
one than we had before—a single 13,500 BTU air conditioner with a heat strip. The heating will come
from the generator engine through insulated pipes to
connector units with thermostatic controlled fan motors that will heat the body.

On occasion, we have used both body doors on the
big one (usually for medical testing and this sort
of thing), but the new one will have only one body
door. We find in most instances that the rear body
door has not been necessary. There will only be one
body door and it will be equipped with a storm door
outside so that the main door can be kept open. The
door inside the vehicle will be kept open and the
storm door will keep out the weather. We added that
to the first truck later. We need that for screens.
You have to keep the door inside the vehicle open.
You can't work with it closed and it is not made to
be opened and closed constantly. The storm door is

aluminum, a regular-looking household door. It is more inviting to people.

The glass projection screen in the side has a problem, in that people who look at a movie also see their own reflection. On the new one we're angling the glass in, at a sufficient angle so that the overhead hood opens up to shield the screen. We'll paint the inside of that flat black so that the only reflection you see will be the underside of a flat black hood. There will be no reflections in the glass. The glass will lean in at about a 10- or 11-degree angle. It's about a 6-inch offset at the top and we will put our rear projection screen, in turn, inside of that.

DR: I noticed that you went for a big generator on that first one. Has it proved to be sufficient? Have you had any generator problems?

JM: We were dealing with a local vendor. We found that the generator didn't work. It never overheated, but it was giving us trouble; it kept spraying out oil. We decided to go to the manufacturer with it. Now that the manufacturer has serviced it we haven't had any more problems. There is one inherent problem with the Onan generator that we use. It has a large air-cooled engine that is noisy, not obtrusively so, but still a pain in the neck. In the new vehicle we are using an Opel. You can hardly tell it is running. The Opel is supplied by Genorak which has been in business for a long time.

DR: Could you give me an idea of the purposes for which your vehicle has been used?

JM: It's been used as a telephone company business office on the street where we handle bill and rate explanations, take complaints, and sell merchandise. As a salesmobile, it has been effective, especially in shopping centers. We also make stops on street corners where there's a high traffic level. It has been in demand for health testing because people like the accessibility, and because it's got plenty of power on board   Health to operate equipment. There's a john large   Testing enough for people to change their clothes in and there's enough lie-down space elsewhere for blood and time tests. People really don't have to lie down for these,

but sickle cell people like to lie down when they're
giving blood samples.

I think that the big unit has been very successful. We had spring trouble with it at first that had
to be corrected. The new one won't be quite as heavily loaded, because we're not putting as much furni-
ture inside of it. It will have a little more floor
space. The display side has worked out very well; we
are able to open the side up and almost literally
put on a show or give a talk right from the unit.
We've shown movies, we've shown videotapes. I think
that this would be something you could use for your
summer programs.

DR: I think that we're going to see more vehicles
like this come out of libraries, but they're a little
slow.

JM: The difficulty in most of these units is to
get head room. We were very fortunate with this new
one. I don't know whether it's going to continue or
not, but the Ford Motor Company, up until a year or
so ago, was going into the motor home business. When
the gas situation came on they backed out before
they got in too deep. As you know, GM got in all the
way. What Ford had left over was a lot of
chassis, but that was all. So they turned
the chassis over to certain body makers   Chassis
and just said, "Do what you can with them."
Boyertown came up with their MS series of
delivery vans. The only difference in these
chassis and the standard Ford chassis (or
Dodge chassis or even Chevy chassis) is
that it will go under a Boyertown 8-foot
wide delivery van. The driver's position is shifted
slightly forward. You have a decent size engine, a
very large fuel tank, and all power options.

You can get an automatic transmission delivery
van. You can automatically get power brakes. For
some reason or other, truck builders just don't put
power steering in. You need that if women are going
to drive the vehicle. Women drive mine, and they
will be driving the new one.

Those new chassis were 1974 models. I don't
know if they are going to keep making them available
but that was a great advantage. To give you the con-
trast, the first truck that we bought, despite its
enormous size, had a relatively small 318 cubic V-8

engine and a 15 gallon gas tank. The new one has got
a 390 cubic engine and a 50 gallon gas tank. That's
the difference between having a motor home chassis
and a van chassis. The motor home chassis comes with
very wide front axles that are not standard on regular delivery vans. This unit was meant to be a wide
vehicle, where the other one had to be adapted and
does not have the stability that this one will have.
It sounds like a lot of technical gibberish, but it
makes a big difference in how the vehicle works on
the road, because wherever you go with it, you've
got to drive it there first.

DR: That's very valuable as far as I'm concerned,
because women will be driving library vehicles. Power steering is very important. Can you think of anything else that's good or bad on this vehicle?

JM: We're sticking with the carpet tiles which
have worked out very well. We used Cullen power bond
tiling, which is incredible stuff. It was so dirty
it looked like it would never recover, yet we got it
shampooed and it came up like new. Cullen power bond
tiling is extremely expensive. It comes in 18-inch
square tiles and costs about $60 per box. The tiles
are glued down just around the corners. If a tile is
damaged, rather than take up the whole carpet, you
either use a cookie cutter to take a circle out from
where it's damaged or you just take the tile out and
put another down. It has proved to be extremely durable.

We've stuck with the Michelin tires, which have
been a godsend under most circumstances.

DR: Any other problems?

JM: As much as I like Winnebago for their willingness to build you what you want, I feel that the
Winnebago is just too delicate a vehicle. You're
talking about a very thin aluminum skin backed up by
foam, backed up with 1/8-inch plywood. We've put
heavy duty aluminum skirts on ours to keep it from
being damaged where it most likely will be damaged.
It's just too delicate. You're better off with a
truck.

DR: You showed me a photo of three people playing
instruments outside the vehicle. How do concerts
like this happen?

JM: That's a block party. We went for an extremely high quality stereo sound system, a Kenwood 6000 amplifier with speakers built into the vehicle. The city of New York, for instance, has a shellmobile that is not nearly in as much demand as ours because their sound system stinks.

GERSTENSLAGER

Ed Howard

"The big thing that's needed is understanding the philosophy of the operation. There needs to be an attitudinal change in the operators. They must develop an ability to work with the community in strange and unfamiliar ways on unfamiliar turf, without seeing any immediate result. It takes a couple of years before you start getting the payoff."

Ed Howard is director of the Vigo County Library in Indiana and a well-known innovator in public library services. He and Harmon Boyd converted an old van for media-ized mobile service, then refined and extended their ideas for a custom-designed unit built by Gerstenslager.

EH: I think probably our definition of media machine is quite different from others. I see it as a vehicle for sending staff, informational materials, and equipment out into the community and working with groups. Take videotape equipment, for example. We might help a neighborhood group in the inner city that really is scared of videotape. The group starts with no idea how they can use it. You take the equipment out and, over a period of time, work with them to where they start being creative on their own. Maybe they even reach a point where they borrow a Sony portapack or at least take the initiative and say, "Hey, we've got a breakfast program that we got to get taped." So this is the way that I see the bookmobile—I don't care what size it is—being used, rather than as a traveling showmobile, with a stage or rear screen projector on the side.

Working with Groups

DR: So you don't play anything back on this machine and you don't check out any materials from it?

EH: Yes, we do, but that is more the traditional use of the vehicle. We go to a neighborhood stop out in the country and there's probably a half dozen elderly people there who look forward to these visits. They come in and get their westerns, novels, gardening information, or whatever. It's only in working with groups on a preplanned, long-term basis that we can really develop the kind of use of the library resources and staff that we're after.

DR: What do you recommend to people to avoid their getting into trouble when they are converting a machine from a conventional one to a media vehicle?

EH: We found no problem whatsoever; we just decided what we wanted to carry on it. It was essentially just having it work and making sure that it fitted our present equipment and what we anticipated in the way of future equipment. We were thinking about projection screens, holders and doors, and some things we could lock, since for the first time we might have things we might want to lock up. I see no problem whatsoever.

DR: Okay, do you have any information people can send for, if they are interested in the details of what you did?

EH: Yes, they could write to Harmon Boyd, coordinator of Extension Services here, and he can send the drawing. If we don't have exactly what people would need, we will be glad to make it up.
    The big thing that's needed is understanding the philosophy of the operation. There needs to be an attitudinal change in the operators. They must develop an ability to work with the community in strange and unfamiliar ways on unfamiliar turf, without seeing any immediate result. It takes a couple of years before you start getting the payoff and, for a year at least, it's discouraging.

DR: What staff did you assign to the unit, besides Harmon?

EH: Harmon was in charge. Then there was Betty Dodson, a white, middle-aged, professional person who is deeply sensitive. This situation was new to

her; she didn't know a thing about video or audio
tape, but she has learned along with the users. Maybe that is one thing that has made our project so
successful.

DR: Have you made a videotape of the machine itself?

EH: No, but there's no reason why we couldn't make
one. If we get enough requests we would make one. We
have some tapes of some of our programs, and we
could edit a tape so people could see what the media
program is all about.

Paul Lawrence

"When you get your first set of blueprints, go
over them very, very carefully because the mediamobile is new to you. If you want something in there,
check those prints . . . because the designers make
errors."

Paul Lawrence was the director of the Daniel
Boone Regional Library in Columbia, Missouri, at the
time this study was done. He believed that mobile
media vehicles were essentially program vehicles,
and that circulation was best kept separate as another mobile function.

DR: It looks like you modified the Weston Woods machine. Could you tell me what the nature of the modifications are, what you consider the improvements to
be, and also what problems you've had with it?

PL: We put a handicap lift in the back. I think
Weston Woods had a school bus that they had modified.
This unit is more like our regular bookmobile. We
left off the outside tables because we didn't know
what this would work into. We still have the inside
projector. We have inside tables.

DR: Is this a modular arrangement?

PL: Yes. We still have the puppet stage, the cur-
tains, the cabinets; these are rearranged a little
bit from Weston Woods, I believe.

DR: What problems have you had with your vehicle?

PL: A few minor problems are all: the air conditioner, for one. We backed into a post and the lift

came loose because they had failed to weld one corner of it. We repaired it in the shop that does our work. The engine has done very well. It needed some adjusting after break-in, since they had run it at too high a speed. One of the drivers hit a big calf and tore up the front end, but that had nothing to do with the unit.

DR: Do you have the unit serviced by the manufacturer of the chassis, or do you take it to someone else?

PL: We have it serviced by the manufacturer, International Harvester.

DR: What would you do differently if you were going to build another mediamobile?

PL: I believe the stage could be constructed a little bit better. I think it's a little bit wide for puppets. You need a narrow stage, and one low enough that children sitting on the floor can see. The projector is also a little bit tight against the wall; it has a thermostat that's very close to a light, and this puts out enough heat that it affects the thermostat. These are relatively minor things that could be worked over easily.

Puppet Stage

DR: What exactly caused you to turn to Gerstenslager?

PL: We've had six of their bookmobiles and they've always done an excellent job. To me they are the finest of the bookmobile builders. They are easy to work with and will do anything any way that you want it done.

DR: Is there anything else you would like to tell a person who might build a mediamobile—any kind of advice?

PL: When you get your first set of blueprints, go over them very, very carefully, because the mediamobile is new to you. If you want something in there, check in the prints, because the designers make errors. For instance, I caught one on a floor they had to raise. They only raised it back to the wheel housing. This left a step off at the back that they didn't notice. They realized that they

had to raise this, and they modified it right away
by running the raised floor the full length of the
unit. That would be my first thing: check those
prints very closely.

DR: How were the specifications made originally?
Did you do this yourself?

PL: The specs were made up the the engineer, Paul
Wire.

DR: You say you have six bookmobiles. Do you see
adding more bookmobiles or do you see this as a
compromise between bookmobiles and mediamobiles?

PL: It can't be a compromise at all. It would be
one or the other. Because of the type of programming, the bookmobile is strictly a service unit for
book materials. I don't see it as a supply vehicle
for media software. It will be used for programming
and teaching.

Linda Knutson

"Our operation is pretty flexible. We don't
have regular stops, so at one point we're trying to
attract black adolescents, at another point we're
trying to attract old street people, derelicts. It
changes from stop to stop."

Linda Knutson was in charge of the Whole World
media vehicle when it began operation at the San
Francisco Public Library. She saw it through its
early days of troubleshooting and program development.

DR: How can people who want to go into media machines avoid mistakes? What advice do you have to
give?

LK: From the technical standpoint,
make the machine as flexible as pos-
sible. We have a monster that's too   Flexibility
heavy to take some places and too tall
to take other places. Nothing was designed with any purpose in mind. The
people who designed it had never done
anything like that before and had never
worked with outreach projects. Although we got a
fairly good product for what we put into it, the

people who were working on the street should have
been the ones involved in designing it. I've never
liked "Whole World." The nebulous name meant nothing
to anyone. It looked like some truck pulling something; it has Madison Avenue graphics on it that
don't say anything about the library. Everyone was
so paranoid about calling themselves a library: they
were sure people would run away from it. I think people think we're selling something and they don't
come in anyway.

DR: What problems did you have? How would you cau-
tion people against specific problems?

LK: Make sure the thing is accessible to all kinds
of people; small children and old people who can't
step up high. Make it safe for them. We've also had
problems with young people in the driver's area. The
gear shift is not closed off and protected, and the
kids are constantly playing with it, which can be a
lot of fun for the kids, but it's very dangerous in
a city as hilly as this. If the emergency brake goes,
it could kill someone. There wasn't anything that
could fold down over it to make it into a work area.

The book racks should be placed so that the book
covers are facing outward, so that people can browse.
(We've stayed completely with paperback material on
the mediamobile.) You can also hang books on the
side, put hooks on the outside of the van and put up
book racks, posters, or bulletin boards, or whatever
you want depending on where you're going. Our operation is pretty flexible. We don't have regular stops,
so at one point we're trying to attract black adolescents, at another point we're trying to attract old
street people, derelicts. It changes from stop to
stop.

DR: Did it work well in rough weather?

LK: We don't have rough weather here. We had a wind
tunnel effect because we wanted the second door on
the back rather than on the side, so that people
could see what was going on. It was more spacious,
but it was more windy. If you were building in the
Midwest, you would have to have better heating.

DR: What about the screen on the side? Could that
be watched in the winter time?

LK: We haven't yet put a protective awning on it,

under which people could stand. Again,
we don't have trouble with rain or with
winter. The main problem with the screen   Exterior
is sun. The booth is not completely dark   Film
and the standard 16mm projector does not   Projection
have a strong enough projection lamp to
project a good image unless it's at night.
In order to get a good image in the day,
I understand there is a projector that
takes a much higher power projection lamp that would
give you good image in daylight. Unless you have the
right combination of shade and lack of glare hitting
that screen, you never have a good image during the
day. It can be all right, but it can be really bad,
too.

DR: What other advice do you have for someone who
might be going into this?

LK: I think it's a pretty good idea to find out
what the public wants before you take it to them.
Make your buying as simple as possible, so that you
can pick up materials immediately. Don't get hung up
in a bureaucracy where it would have to go through
several departments in the library. Get direct buying from dealers and distributors. That will allow
you to respond to immediate needs. Within a week you
can get a load of new materials if you need it. Your
public is constantly changing and is not as constant
as those you'll find in a branch or main library.
You have to keep yourself as flexible as possible on
every level.

DR: What about the machine itself?

LK: We had the audio for the film coming out on
the outside of the van. We also had a stereo tuner
that we could play in or outside or both. We were
supposed to have a tape recorder hooked up to that,
but it never worked out. Again, flexibility is the
key. You need to be able to be inside, outside, or
both depending on the situation. The speaker for the
projector was initially tied into the speakers that
would project the sound from the tuner outside. We
discovered it was supposed to be hooked up to a little speaker near the bottom close to the screen, but
that wasn't enough. It should be designed so the
sound comes from somewhere near the screen or above
it. The sound only came from the right side of the

truck and not the other side. If you were using the
vehicle to attract people from all sides by sound,
let's say in a playground area, it wouldn't work
because the speakers were set up only on the street
side of the truck. When the truck was parked it
wouldn't hurt to have speakers going outside from
all sides of the truck.

BOYERTOWN

Dan Duran

"We began programming beforehand. . . . We went
mobile without the machine. One thing people trying
to put together machines and programs should know
is the importance of starting the program immediately. Use anything! We used city jeeps, city trucks,
city utility trucks, and borrowed the bookmobile
whenever possible. We would go out and take portable
rear projection screens, draw power from a house or
day care center, and show films. We started the program without the unit. The message was being spread
as we got out survival information on VD, food
stamps, legal aid, etc. We realized that everything
need not hinge upon the vehicle."

Dan Duran was in charge of Outreach at the
Richmond (California) Public Library at the time
this study was done. His involvement in the building
of the media vehicle for RPL was from a "nuts and
bolts" perspective. He offers real insights for
those who plan to build vehicles themselves.

DD: I will be talking about mediamobiles based
pretty much on my experience from 1971 to 1973 in
designing and supervising a mediamobile for the
Richmond California Public Library. Much was learned
from visits to other mediamobiles and their operators. After serving as a bookmobile librarian to a
machine with limited resources, it was a joy to vis-
it remodeled mobile units or new mobile units that
were equipped with print and audiovisuals.
The first lesson learned in pursuing the potential of the mediamobile was that there were few pro-
totypes operating. Some of the best were personally
designed by the librarians, drivers, and clerks who

would later operate them. It took only a short time
to realize that the design of our mediamobile would
begin with the aid of those who already had practical experience. I made visits to the three mediamobile operators in the Bay Area. We talked about generator platforms, shoreline cables, lighting, shelving, and numerous other problems.

I learned that there is a great willingness to
tell other people about the mistakes made before the
entire operation got rolling. For instance, when I
went over to Berkeley, not only did I just go check
out the vehicle and take pictures of it—I rode in
it. We talked about the need for heavy-duty suspension, since most existing units had heavy rear view
projection units on board and carried a lot of equipment. Weight load, the center of gravity, and other
matters were also discussed. I soon realized that
mediamobiles were not a novelty to their promoters.
For those who had experimented with existing units
or designed new ones, the time of the mediamobile
had arrived.

I remember talking to Dave Gutman at
a California Library Association confer-
ence 6 months before my shell came. He   The First
said that he had experimented with the   Mediamobile
mediamobile 15 years before anyone really
thought of anything other than the traditional bookmobile. He gutted a vehicle
from the inside and fashioned a makeshift
rear screen projection booth. He blacked out the
windows to show movies inside by day. But only a few
people supported the idea then and he couldn't con-
vince them that this was the way to go.

DR: How did you go about planning your vehicle?

DD: Checked out what had already been done. A lot
of mediamobiles have been built with federal or
state money, and frequently the blueprints or plans
are available. I wrote a stipulation into our particular project that the plans would be available to
anyone who was interested in them and that a small
sum be set aside for furnishing these plans. I believed our vehicle would be a prototype from which
other people could learn. We had to push this
through the city council. Why should anyone hoard a
solution to a common problem and keep it to themselves? After all, we had learned from others: at

the early construction stage, we had help from people like Linda Knutson at San Francisco Public and
Ed Minczenski from Berkeley Public Library. We were
in continuous contact with each other. I frequently
attended talks about regular bookmobile service.

About this time, bookmobilers and extension service heads were beginning their own mobile unit con-
versions. A lot of people were simultaneously considering the best ways to design new units. The California Library Association invited a number of us to
form a chapter of Extension Services. One of the
first things we did was to say, let's look and share
with each other. The chapter had one meeting in Richmond while we were still building our own machine
and people were able to check on what was happening
with our unit. Another time we had a
mediamobile caravan during a chapter
meeting. It was our Northern Califor-   Mediamobile
nia contingent and since we believed   Caravan
in working programs, we had almost a
dozen mobile units around the city
hall square, all available for inspec-
tion by the public and librarians.
There was bedlam, with people walking
in and out of them saying, "Man, the plexiglass dome
on top of the mediamobile is really where it's at!
and "Look at how the light is diffused!" Minczenski
noted, "Look, this generator isn't so bad if you
fiberglass the inside of the hood. It's a good,
cheap power system." People were comparing Onan and
Kohler generators, asking each other, "What sort of
mileage are you getting on board these things?"
Those who were starting had an opportunity to learn
from the past.

Mediamobiles are often made from old bookmobile
bodies. Some are totally new and designed from
scratch. Flexibility goes hand in hand with mediamo-
bility; because of that almost everything you do
will be an innovation. It's going to be a new device
or instrument to use out in the street.

DR: What about costs?

DD: The city librarian, city officials, and state
library people were all concerned about costs. If we
had decided to send off to Gerstenslager, who charges
a buck or two a pound, we might not have been happy
with the product. We decided to use our own city man-

power, the corporation yard, city engineer, city
carpenters, and city welders. When we started having
to pay them too much, we found other sources, like
the community college. So all through the planning
stage, I talked to many people about developing the
machine. It didn't come out as an "immaculate con-
ception"; there was the input from other machines,
from the people who have been driving vehicles and
thinking about ways to construct them. There was a
lot of grass roots input from the city fathers down
to local community groups.

One of the first things we did was show pictures
of vehicles to the city fathers and the public, because many found it difficult to imagine a mediamobile. Was it a bookmobile or a roving TV station?
What was this thing the library intended to build?
We found that the best way to proceed was to show
them pictures, give them a slide show, and then sell
the mediamobile idea. During our presentations we
would find some people whose eyes would light up.
One engineer in particular was quite excited and
said he was tired of the drab work that he did for
the city engineering department. We took him aside
because we knew we'd get better work from him. We
explained our budget problems to him and said that
we did not want our unit planned somewhere else, in
a factory.

We were trying to cut costs. On the basis of our
funds and what had been done successfully before, we
thought we'd try our own hand. We had initially
planned on $45,000 for two years (from an LSCA [Li-
brary Services and Construction Act] grant). It
would give us $25,000 the first year and $20,000 the
second year and would cover machines, materials, and
manpower. We should have realized that the costs of
constructing the final vehicle would equal, if not
surpass, the cost of the chassis alone. Then there
was the cost of salaries and the fringe benefits and
the materials. We didn't really quite know what we
were getting into in terms of costs. We had a vague
idea, but we just couldn't put an estimated dollar
amount on the mediamobile unit itself.

The city engineer said that he could not keep up
with the waves of blueprints we kept changing as we
went along. We convinced the carpenters, the electri-
cians, all our workers, to be innovative by saying,
"Here's basically what we want, and here's what's

been done before. Look at the blueprints, but don't
stick to them: do it better yourself." They did! We
realized that a lot of it had to come from their own
individual talents, from the pride of people in
their jobs. When it came to the rear projection
booth, the carpenter said that this was the toughest
thing he had ever had to do because of the structural constraints of the van. He built a beautiful
booth with his own plans.

There were few prepackaged materials because
there was no single supplier for the electrical system, the cabinets, the projection system, or whatever. Everything had to be ordered in advance. The
planning had to be done as quickly as possible to
allow for receipt of materials on schedule. To begin
with, we needed a shell. We went to truck
companies to determine the best chassis
for our needs. Someone suggested a mon-   Body
ster camper van and we were shown campers   Strength
that were so light we could punch dents
into the side. What do you think would
have happened if we had hit the side of
a tree? Everybody was convinced of the
need for sturdiness and maneuverability,
and the need not to frighten people. We did not want
to be mistaken for a paddy wagon or an X-ray van.

Size was considered. We wanted about 13½ feet of
loading space, with about 5 feet in front. When we
went to dealers, we had a vague idea of what to look
for. We wanted the ceilings inside the vehicle to be
7 feet, but we had to find out exactly what was
available. When we thought about the ceilings, we
also had to consider whether to have light fixtures
that came out 3 or 4 inches or light fixtures that
would be flush. We thought about how high the body
should be inside (the floor space to the ceiling).
We considered the type of lights we were going to
get. Everything was starting to mesh like fingers
interlocking. It became easier to visualize the vehicle. We realized that we didn't want a huge generator system that would power air conditioners and
heating units because we just didn't have the money.
We considered siding and whether insulation was
needed.

We visited various distributors and settled for
Boyertown. They made a variety of special vehicles
and utility trucks. I don't know if they are the

best, but they were the best for our particular program. I don't think there is one best company: they
all will get you whatever chassis you want and make
necessary modifications.

In general, it seems best to find out exactly
what the dimensions of your shell are; get as clear
an idea as possible of what you are going to have
inside of it; know how much weight it's going to
have to carry; and then submit the bids. In our case,
the whole bidding process was a nightmare. There
were the city regulations about three bids, the de-
lays, and signing of the contracts, etc. The big
lesson we learned was to get the delivery date in
writing, since it was a full year after our funding
before we had our machine on the road. A full year's
an outrageous amount of time.

We began programming beforehand. In
other words, we went mobile without the
machine. One thing people trying to put   Programming
together machines and programs should   without
know is the importance of starting the   a Vehicle
program immediately. Use anything! We
used city jeeps, city trucks, city
utility trucks, and borrowed the bookmobile whenever possible. We would go out and take
portable rear projection screens, draw power from a
house or day care center, and show films. We used
the LSCA money and bought materials, particularly
films. The regular film collection grew and we began
our own film shows. We started our program without
the unit. The message was being spread as we got out
survival information on VD, food stamps, legal aid,
etc. We realized that everything need not hinge upon
the vehicle. Multimedia would really give our program a shot in the arm and make it electric, but the
machine wasn't everything. We spent the money and we
ordered material. Some people asked why we were ordering the mirror six months before it would be
ready to put in. I replied that we wanted it ready
when the time came. So one other suggestion I have—
order in advance. Order everything for your machine
that will possibly be needed. We ordered our rear
view projection mirror four months before they
thought we needed it. It was two months late in coming and arrived almost exactly as the machine was
ready to go. It was a good thing we ordered when we
did.

Our standard procedure was to go in person to
each vendor and say, "Look, here's what we're going
to do." We showed them pictures, gave them the idea,
and had them work it out. Get people committed and
devoted, work on them, go out and drink with them,
be around. I was frequently around the corporation
yard three or four hours a day. I wanted to hear the
problems they ran into on our mobile unit. If I had
to be a lackey and go out and buy a piece of neo-
prene, I'd do it. If someone asked what we were doing about the vent for the generator, I became the
errand person and tracked one down. The critical
thing was to plug into the mobile unit construction
in any possible manner. When you run the machine,
you have to know the guts; you have to know what
makes it tick; you have to know where things are
placed. One of the biggest problems, in terms of
mediamobile operation, is having a ready-made, prepackaged unit without any idea of where the vitals
are or what they look like or how to get to them
when needed.

When we finally received the shell, it was ugly
as sin. People asked how we could possibly do anything with it. It looked like an armored tank vehicle, it was so ugly. We were going to dress it, to
change it, to mold it. The main thing was to make
sure that it was as flexible as possible.

DR: What makes your van different from a bookmobile?

DD: Well, the key thing is obviously media, but
is it enough to have it wired so that people can
plug inside and listen to music, so that it can become a traveling movie house? We decided it was all
in the mix. It sounds corny, but it was half traditional, more or less, and half outrageousness. We
didn't want the conventional resources in there; we
wanted material that would attract people, get them,
hold them. We wanted people to get their hands on
it. Our mediamobile philosophy is that the unit can
be used and touched by everyone.

DR: What kind of construction theory did you follow?

DD: Construction was modular. If something happened to our rear view projection screen, we wanted
to have a large portable screen that we could take

out and put beneath an awning and use.
Everything had to be able to come in
and out and everyone had to be able to   Modular
use the equipment. We just didn't want   Construction
to be like a large magnet enticing peo-
ple to sell them the regular library
line.
     We told ourselves that we knew some
of the needs because we were from the community. In
the regular bookmobile you're supposed to know the
community. Bookmobile staffs provide a great and wonderful service; they can and do offer specialized
and extensive services. But the mediamobile needs in-
digenous people, people who talk the lingo, who rap,
who know street talk. It may be the one spot in all
library service where you have to speak the language
because people so often feel insecure and intimi-
dated by libraries. You have to get them over that
first hurdle and the staff must do it.

   DR: What problems did you have?

   DD: A major problem was with the generator. We couldn't figure out a good
way to make it serviceable. A number of   Electrical
heavy-duty generators are useful. A lot   Power
of generating plants can really be cut
down. Conserve your energy and get it
cheaper. A 2500 watt generator is mini-
mum for a machine that's going to have
to power a couple of projectors, a stereo system perhaps, and its own lighting system. With 5000 watts
you can do a lot of fancy things, both inside and
outside the machine. One reason for having a generator with more power than needed for daily operations
is for programs where you supply power to other people or groups. We mounted our generator on a removable platform that was bolted down so that we could
just drop out the whole generator. We had a 110/220
watt auxiliary power line installed into our breaker
box to solve that problem. There were other problems
regarding the electrical system, the projection system, and the lights, but most things related to the
generator system. Because it must be quiet, you must
have exterior generator mufflers. You must be able
to make the decision, too, when not to use it. With
the 110/220, I would try to hook into a house or a
utility pole that the bookmobile used, rather than

using my own generator. The hookup will give all the power needed with no generator noise. The generator vibrates when it runs and people sometimes reacted to the rumbling inside the vehicle. This can be distracting if you haven't insulated the generator compartment well. We built a seat on top of our generator compartment (which also held a spare tool chest underneath it), so that people could sit on it. We thought that this was sort of snappy because no space was left unused.

DR: Can you tell me about the mistakes you think you made?

DD: I've already mentioned one, in terms of ordering the body. I did not enforce the stipulation of the contract on how long they had to deliver it. In terms of the actual body itself, even with the paint, the add-ons and the transformation that was made with the shelves and the machines, it still looked too much like an armored truck. Paint does a lot, antennae wires do a lot, exterior shelves do a lot, but it's still not "soft" enough. Somehow or other, I think there should be a softness to it.

Another thing we should have anticipated was the door problem. People have all sorts of ideas about doors. I wanted   Door
a rear and a front opening. We got that   Problems
front opening all right, but it was one
of these regular openings that delivery
vans use. We had to slide the right seat
forward to maximize entrance space. We
should have found another body with the door in the center. As for the rear doors, I'm still not sure. Ours has two half-doors that open all the way so that we could put an aluminum set of steps on the frame similar to the Berkeley mediamobile. If the machine gets too large, it's really hard to keep an eye on what's happening. There must be some way of reducing the space needed by the rear view projection booth so you can have a clear view and have two side doors instead of just a rear door and a front door.

I should have purchased things sooner than I did. I was convinced by other people to hold off. Why spend all your money for a stereo or a projector when you don't even have the chassis here yet? But we could have used the equipment earlier. We did use

what we had in senior citizen centers and other
places. My mistake was in waiting so long. I should
have gone out and spent all that I had allocated for
material and equipment purchases. I also should have
consulted other mediamobilers who had warned me
about their own mistakes. If I had someone there,
like Ed Miczenski of Berkeley, who knew the problems,
it would have gone much quicker. We should have developed a consultant file.

I really wanted to have natural light,
as much natural light as possible. I should
have installed more plexiglass or fiber-   Natural
glass domes. The Berkeley machine had one   Lighting
such light dome. There is a niceness about
having this round thing letting light into
this rectangular machine. I'm convinced of
the power and beauty of natural light and
I think that people really like to be able
to look out.

I couldn't afford an air conditioner. They are a
luxury except in places that are hot all the time. I
wanted to have cassette racks built in so that if I
had a lot of cassettes, I could store them in the
rear view projection booth. I didn't ask for them because of other priorities. My advice is to get everything on the unit that you think you are going to
need. But be careful; a cluttered machine scares people off. In terms of a rear view projection booth,
we didn't waste any space on it. What we did was to
build a level table upon which the projector sat. We
made cabinets underneath the table cabinet that
would slide out for storage of materials. We could
then store our projector permanently on board the
mediamobile. There were two doors mounted on slide
rails with bearings. These doors, which we covered
with a porous material, acted as walls to shut off
light inside the projector booth built atop the level table top.

DR: How has the vehicle held up? Is it shaking
down to pieces or has it stayed tight? What's the
maintenance factor on it?

DD: The maintenance factor hasn't been too bad.
The crews have only seen it four times. I've been on
board it a couple of times since I left the outreach
program and I'm disappointed that it's exactly as I
left it. The fact that very few things have been

changed can mean one of two things: one, that it was
built in such a way that it works; or two, people
just haven't gotten around to improving and fixing
it. I talked to the corporation yard people who had
it in for its regular generator maintenance. They
said it was good that we had the generator built so
it could be taken off if we needed our auxiliary power system or 110/220. They thought the generator
would supply enough power.

The paint has held up fantastically in terms of
splotches and scratches and such. I don't remember
the paint mixture, but they said it wouldn't rust
and if scratches got on it, it would be easy to re-
paint. The paint job is simple and nice. We had the
colors we wanted and I think the sum is a combination of life and life's tempo. In terms of its exterior appearance, it's been okay.

DR: Do you need special training for people to
work on your vehicles? Sometimes a bookmobile crew
put on a mediamobile feels lost.

DD: I wanted to have the crew I had on my bookmobile work on my mediamobile because I knew they were
different. I knew I worked well with them and I
wanted the bookmobile people not to have professional jealousies. I wanted them to know both operations,
to be able to substitute. We think of our mediamobile as not replacing the bookmobile; it simply has
different functions. We would call and help each
other out whenever we had to.

I think you are going to get into
more unusual, curious, exciting, and
adventurous experiences in the media-   Visibility
mobile than on a bookmobile or in a   of the
branch. You're going to see more and   Mediamobil
get around more. You're going to be
more visible. People are going to be
hitting on you. You have to be much
cooler about things. I think maybe in
one word, mediamobile people have to be very "cool"—
the coolest workers the library has. Some of our
best workers are New York City kids who are part of
our nuclear community workers.

One thing that we decided, too, was that everyone had to rotate. That is part of my philosophy
about the mediamobile trip: everyone has to rotate
and do the dull work as well as the exciting work.

Everyone has to have the chance to turn on the projector, give the little talk, show someone the machine, help with a library card, whatever it may be.

DR: What about production? I know that you're into
half-inch videotape. What is your philosophy of production in media vehicles?

DD: I don't think production on the
mediamobile has a single purpose. I
think it's multipurposeful. One of the   Production
reasons that we did production was for   on the
training. We wanted to train people   Mediamobile
not just in the library, but in the
community—the contact people—the
woman who headed the day care center,
the people at the senior citizens center, those people who were involved in community organizations and
needed machinery and equipment. We wanted to make
sure that everyone who used our stuff was as compe-
tent as they could be. Our number one concern was
the production of abilities.

In terms of actual media production, I don't
know if there is time. We used half-inch and put it
on over the local cable station. We broadcast a series of programs: legal aid in Spanish, VD, and
Planned Parenthood. We had several reasons for doing
that: first, to let the organizations in town know
that we were doing things and make them aware that
we had equipment and some capabilities to help them.
We didn't try to snow them with our expertise, because we couldn't do it all, but we did want them to
know that we were there. It was also fantastic public relations for the library, so it served that
function as well. And it introduced many people to
the library for the first time.

Production could be production for your own unit
and your own programs or for others and their own
programs. We did very simple things, and we weren't
elegant. We had a couple of work/study library
school students teach day care people how to make
their own filmstrips. These were very simple, basic
things that everyone can do for very little money.
Kids were taught how to use cameras; we bought a
couple of cameras for the project. We wanted the
kids to be able to take pictures of their areas.
When we stopped by, we would have a little photo-
graphic display to let them know we knew what their

area was like, too. We say that production is good
for public relations, it's good for contact, it's
good to let people know that you are around. But
it's hard to know when to stop. The more credence,
legitimacy, and visibility you get in the community,
in terms of their acceptance of your knowledge and
ability to teach them how to do things, the more you
are asked to do. It's one of those laws. We got to
the point where the more successful we were, the
more energy and the more pressure were being put on
us. We had to learn how to say "no." That seems like
a really general thing to say about production, to
learn when to say "no." At one time we were thinking
about having a young filmmakers' special like San
Francisco Public did. We would have it with our mediamobile to show the regular library that our kids
knew where it was at, too. We worked on it for three
months, but couldn't do it ourselves. We trained the
parks and recreation people how to use the cameras
and to act as the kids' support system.

   I think the most important tool we can use is videotape. People love seeing themselves. It may be a
novelty that wears off for a good percentage of them,
but for a lot of others it's a high. The Adult Basic
Education and English as a Second Language programs
use it for teaching purposes. It was really a great
functional tool for them. For kids aged 13 to 19, it
became a skill they developed and were proud of.

   DR: Where do you see all this going? If you were a
library director and you had some money, where would
you put it for mobile service?

   DD: First of all, I would start a massive public
relations campaign within the library. I would want
to sell my own staff first because I would like my
staff supporting it. I would not want them thinking
I was disrupting or prostituting the library. I
would want them to think that this was going to en-
large upon the library, that it would bring in more
beauty and excitement. Everyone would have a say in
it and everyone would have a chance to help plan.

   One of the first things with mediamobiles is
that they can't and they shouldn't operate the way
a regular library does. All the way from registra-
tion to circulation, to shelving, to materials, to
programming, they are different.

   I would like to create a fleet of them if I had
the money.

CHINOOK

Dave Gutman

"We produced video. We produced audio. I looped
the inside of the mobile unit so we had both open
and closed sound simultaneously. We produced stuff
in five languages."

Dave Gutman worked for the San Diego County
(California) Library at the time this study was done.
His outreach project gave strong emphasis to video
production and playback.

DR: Could you describe your vehicle, not so much
in terms of service patterns, but as a physical
entity?

DG: I was hedged in by the nature of the project.
I was obligated to experiment and demonstrate, which
I wanted to do. I tried to determine what I was going to do with the mediamobile in terms of service,
and what range was needed. I considered the kind of
terrain I would be covering and how long we'd be out.
All these factors influenced the design, and money
did too. One of the problems was that there was nothing like it around. I just decided I would get a
blank vehicle, a 27-foot Chinook body on a Dodge
frame and get it peg-boarded. Then I'd design the
rest of the stuff, as modules that all fit together.

DR: What was right and what was wrong with that
solution?

DG: Well, the solution was okay for me but I didn't
go far enough with it. I had an awning and I wanted
to snap a tent on to the awning and expand the kind
of service we gave to accommodate 50 or 60 people.
But I didn't have enough staff to do that. I didn't
go far enough. I also wanted to experiment with the
idea that the library is not just a storer and re-
triever of information, but a producer of special
information for special needs. That's how I saw this
project. That's what I've been interested in since
I've been around libraries.

DR: How did it work?

DG: It worked well. We produced video, we produced
audio. I looped the inside of the mobile unit so we
had both open and closed sound simultaneously. We

produced stuff in five languages: the three Indian languages, Spanish, and English. I wanted to take it far but I didn't take it far enough. I wanted to get into producing microforms but I didn't have enough people to support that—I needed support for things that were going on, especially in the native American communities on the reservation. The project went on reservations and into barrios and migrant camps.

DR: What equipment was designed into the vehicle?

DG: Everything that we had in the vehicle could be used either as a part of the vehicle (equipment could be assembled for a whole media show) or removed from the vehicle. We had nothing built in. I didn't want a built-in screen because it took up too much space. I used rear screen projection on a cart. I ordered the cart from the Midwest. A very large screen is strapped on to the cart and wheeled down a ramp. Then the cart wheels are locked and the screen is strapped onto the side of the vehicle. I bolted down projectors and all that to the cart. I had other carts for the video gear and also super-8, 16mm, synched filmstrip and cassette, as well as paperbacks.

Removable Equipment

DR: How did you handle power? What kind of generator did you have?

DG: I had the biggest Onan generator built and discovered that I should have had better load leveling for producing video. I had to go to the battery for video. I discovered that it's essential to get the Onan serviced after every 100 hours of use. I very carefully logged the service time and made a service contract with an Onan dealer. I felt that was very important and I still do.

DR: And Dodge serviced the rest of it?

DG: Because of the limitations of the funding, I was stuck to certain fiscal agents: in the case of the vehicle, I was saddled with a bureaucratic servicing from one of the government agencies for the first year. The second year I made a contract with Dodge. I tried to get it the first year but couldn't. I think it would have been important and that's a good question.

DR: Tell me what happened: What do you think caused the demise? Was it the federal funding?

DG: It was an LSCA project and funding ran out. That meant that the service just terminated and nobody picked it up.

DR: So the vehicle is sitting in a parking lot somewhere and the gear is stored?

DG: I have heard that the vehicle is being used as a bookmobile right now for another project.

DR: So the hardware is just stashed away some place?

DG: To the best of my knowledge, yes. Sure, you've got thousands and thousands of dollars worth of hardware. There are a lot of problems and all of these are familiar to you, I'm sure. One problem is if you're dealing with media, you're dealing with media in a book context. It's like what Pauline Kael wrote about film. Film is something you watch in the dark. Media is something you do in the dark, in the library. For me that has very heavy implications. I could spend another three hours on this: it's nothing you don't know.

DR: If you could redesign that vehicle and do it just the way you want, what would you do? Let's say you weren't worried about being shut down in two years because of funding, and you could really do it. What features would be in that vehicle?

DG: If I could do it any way I wanted to I probably would go to the same company that builds the coaches for Greyhound buses. Those are $100,000 rigs. There is at least one bookmobile in California that cost around $85,000 that has to be moved by a tractor trailer rig. For $100,000 you could get a Greyhound bus and really do a media unit and not worry about it.

DR: What would you have in it?

DG: I would try to install holograms in it and I would try to talk Berkeley or UCLA into some cooperative experimental program for information storage, retrieval, and production in holograms. In addition to microforms and all other media, I would keep paperbacks. In the LSCA project, I drop loaded a lot

of stuff. I also circulated all of
the hardware of my project, which I
think is an important factor. I cir-   Circulating
culated projection equipment, all   Video
the video equipment, everything. I   Equipment
circulated it to somebody in the com-
munity with whom I had an agreement,
like the tribal council on the reservation. From there, they did what-
ever they wanted to do with the equipment. The film,
projectors, videotape, cameras, recorder, whatever.

DR: How did it work?

DG: Great. Losses on hardware were zero, damage to
hardware was zero, and my book losses were consider-
ably lower on the honor system. No library cards. On
the honor system losses are much, much lower than in
the average library system. It works but you have to
have some understanding established to make it work.

DR: Bookmobile builders don't seem to have many
ideas. They then run into a library that doesn't
have any ideas either. They both come out with something pretty standard that is locked into the past.

DG: It's safe, too. How do you think these guys
survive? Not by doing the stuff we've been playing
around with. You must establish service goals before
you even begin to discuss hardware and software. Design begins here. Alternatives to bigger rigs would
include soft units (tents, balloon/collapsibles), VW
vans, openbed trucks, etc. All to suit the kind of
service desired.

DR: Have you got any parting shots for potential
mobile vehicle builders?

DG: I didn't know a thing about it before I
started. What I tried to do was go around and ask a
lot of questions. I even visited some of the factories in California. Chinook is diversified and decen-
tralized so they have little factories all over. I
went in and saw how things were made. I talked to
everybody, asked a lot of questions, and then tried
to sort it out. I made a list of what I wanted to do
and what I wanted the machine to do. We had unusual
problems. We had to service mountains, deserts, all
of that. I made a list of the kind of service and
where we would have to go. I often got conflicting

advice. You just have to work it out to the best of your ability, and try to get the best possible advice.

I think the key thing wrong was maintenance. Maintenance is a real hassle. You have to find somebody who is dependable and work out a contract. Also, the bureaucracy tends to be awesome on projects where you have different agents for different things and where you must conform to their buying rules. I found it got in my way because the criteria that the agents set up weren't necessarily the criteria that met my needs. I wanted to project to be open-ended so that I could build. Did you ever try to go in and tell a purchasing agent, "Look, I don't know where it's going to wind up, but. . . ."

Maintenance Problems

DR: Dan Duran mentioned that there was a camaraderie among media vehicles in California. Did you have some event where the vehicles met?

DG: We met at the California Library Association meeting in '72 or '73, appropriately enough at Disneyland. There was a "mobile'in." It was mostly just bookmobiles where people talked things over.

DR: Outside of the San Francisco, Berkeley, Oakland vehicles and your own, are there any other media vehicles in California that are worth mentioning?

DG: I'm not completely sure now. There was an art slide mobile in the San Bernardino desert area funded by a federal grant. Then there was another mobile unit on down towards San Diego, in one of the valleys. That was a music lab, a mobile music lab run by one of the school districts.

WAVE PROJECT

Ed Minczenski

"It takes a pretty still backbone and incredible patience to wrestle a mediamobile from a library board. It's worth it."

Ed Minczenski has been doing AV work and operating the Wave Project media vehicle for the Berkeley

(California) Public Library for several years. He
is one of the "nitty-gritty" pioneers and has consulted on various media vehicles.

DR: If you had to do it over again, what would
you do differently?

EM: There are several systems that have been weak
or performed unsatisfactorily. Our current electric
generator system, mounted in the front of the vehicle, is a high rpm gasoline-powered device that generates much noise and vibration. It has no voltage
metering or regulating system and surges at incon-
venient moments, blowing projector lamps and acces-
sory electrical equipment.

Future generating plants should be placed outside the vehicle, and should be of the low rpm, low
noise-vibration type.

The rear projection system has in-
furiating ambient light problems. The
external shade awning that was designed   Rear
to block out direct overhead illumina-   Projection
tion cannot eliminate ambient light.   System
The screen itself seems to have some
peculiar light-gathering characteristics
that preclude the use of wide-angle
lenses. The large image is too diffuse and
ill defined under sunlight conditions to be satisfactory. At the same time, the shade awning, with
its supporting poles, is often a navigational haz-
ard to passers-by and an attraction to children,
who sometimes swing from it. It may be possible to
eliminate the rear screen projection system completely and still maintain a mobile media unit by
using the U-Matic video cartridge-cassette systems
or some variation on the large rear screen systems,
such as the self-contained Dukane, Technicolor, or
Fairchild portable rear-screen units. Interior
lighting has been a little weak. Our dependence on
110 AC-DC power originally meant that the generator
had to start just to get the lights up for late
afternoon winter operation. That's a waste of fuel
and only adds smoke and noise to the environment.
Future mobilers should use low voltage neon, operated off the van battery, wherever possible.

Operators should choose the cinematic medium
that is best suited to the mobile environment. We
were originally equipped with super-8, 35mm slide,

and 35mm filmstrip projectors and software. In the
last six years I have used these very little, having added 16mm equipment to my inventory. The 16mm
image is more intense, which is essential for out-
of-doors presentations. The resolution of 16mm film
is ridiculously better than super-8. There is also
a lot more available in 16mm than super-8, and in
optical sound as well. It doesn't seem as though the
promised developments in super-8 have occurred or a
standardization of sound systems. Magnetic sound,
optical sound—you have to have an entire AV shop
at your disposal just to preview material. There is
also the conflict in super-8 between reel-to-reel,
cartridge, and cassette.

DR: You mentioned the U-Matic video system.

EM: We don't have the U-Matic system at the moment
and I seriously doubt that we'll ever have it in the
mobile environment. I'm investigating the possibility of installing U-Matics in various branch libraries as satellite AV stations. I'd invite local video
creators to deposit their stuff for local perusal
and exposure. It would create a hands-on environment
in which people could run their own show. There's
just not the room in the Media Machine, given the
projection booth, storage areas, etc., to include
that sort of activity.

DR: What is the size of your unit?

EM: Overall vehicle length is 18 feet, with a loading body of 11 to 12 feet. Interior height is nearly
7½ feet and interior width is 6 feet. I'm pleased
with the size because I'm still a one-man operation.

DR: Would a larger vehicle involve additional
staff?

EM: It might. It might make you think
you needed additional staff. I have no-   Staff
ticed a tendency for bookmobiles to be   Needs
occasionally topheavy with personnel. I
object to larger vehicles on principle.
There's no need for them in most urban
areas. Most large vans are very heavy.
They are made of steel, use double rear
wheels, and have heavy-duty everything. Heavy vehicles sink into warm asphalt in the summer, into snow
in the winter, and into mud in the spring. Long vehi-

les are not maneuverable and space is <u>always</u> a consideration in urban areas.

<u>DR</u>: Describe the Outreach vehicle.

<u>EM</u>: The Berkeley-Oakland Service System received a $120,000 grant from LSCA funds in 1972 to develop an extended services program to certain groups who were, for all practical purposes, outside of the service sphere of either the Berkeley or Oakland library systems. The grant was absurdly omnidirectional. Common sense dictated that we'd have to focus in one area in order to achieve any sort of service continuity and to establish a type of service that could be objectively evaluated. One group which everyone suddenly noticed was the geriatric. As chairman of the Outreach Committee, I was trying to figure out a method of serving the alienated elderly long before <u>Time</u> and <u>Newsweek</u> found out about what wasn't being done for <u>them</u>.

Anyway, we planned to provide multimedia materials for convalescent hospitals in Berkeley and Oakland as a first step toward providing these people with service from public information agencies. I designed a vehicle that would carry these materials around town and we bought a Chevrolet step van with a 14-foot body. It was an all-aluminum, V-8 automatic, stripped vehicle, with full rear doors and a rear hydraulic lift with a 600 pound capacity. The modifications were as follows: full interior paneling, installation of 3x7 skylight, installation of wire book racks and storage cabinets, and design and mounting of modular AV systems. This Outreach vehicle was really just a delivery truck. Its sole purpose was to get people and materials from place to place, from which it would all be an "off the street operation."

Outreach to the Elderly

<u>DR</u>: You did the design and followup?

<u>EM</u>: I was chairman of the committee. I wrote the proposal and researched the whole thing. After we got the grant, I made the modifications I mentioned and I did this with one other person. After I completed the vehicle I was sick of the whole business and went back to the relative comfort of the Media Machine.

DR: Have you followed that thing at all in terms of its success?

EM: The program has been a terrific success, I'm glad to say, because of expanded humanity more than expanded technology. The truck delivers the materials, certainly, but that's less to the truck's credit than to the people who drive it. None of the patients in the convalescent homes ever sees the truck, so its snazzy paint job is fairly irrelevant, for them at least.

The program has been funded by the county along with the state library and private foundations. The county is presently doing some advanced research, along with the university and certain private groups, into the problems of aging.

DR: This approach is similar to Vigo County, Indiana.

EM: You can do anything with a delivery vehicle you want to. You have no on-board problems if you have no on-board people.

DR: I was thinking the same thing.

EM: I've been doing this kind of thing on and off for the last few years. You drop someone or something off, scoot off to a park, school, or street corner and then make the pickup and head off again. You can do whatever you want and have the energy to accomplish, really. That's the only limitation and yet it is a very practical limitation. Dealing with the public can be an exhausting experience and dealing with the elderly can be even more so. But at the same time I find I get a certain energy from each group I deal with—at least I get perspective and encouragement.

DR: Do you know of any similar library vehicles doing community production?

EM: I don't know of anyone doing this. Dave Gutman said he'd been recording dying Indian languages.

DR: What do you think of modular design?

EM: I think modular design is the way to go. The Media Machine is basically a modular vehicle. I should say it has become one over the years. We have portapak capability and have, at times, operated as a video production unit. With a few more videotape recorder (VTR) devices we could go into some advanced production with broadcast medium sophistication.

I also use other AV machinery such as the portable 35mm formats already mentioned, and have always used the modular wire book rack: easy come, easy go.

Yet certain areas have a terrific resistance to the idea of expanded programming. Oakland, for example, is in the process of acquiring several state-funded bookmobiles and they won't hear of making provisions for on-board media.

DR: So they don't even have software checkout?

EM: Apparently not. They are interested in bookmobile operation and sneer at the frivolity of the Media Machine's paint scheme.

DR: What future do you see in this for yourself?

EM: As it stands, at the moment, not a great deal. This is the sort of operation that requires both leadership and money. Unfortunately, for the last four years my budget has barely maintained past levels of service. The program will be maintained, but there will not be much advancement in terms of putting out more vehicles, buying more hardware, software, etc.

DR: If you were to start at a drawing board, what would you do?

EM: Build a fleet. Branch libraries are becoming more and more expensive, little-used prodigals of urban library systems. They are seldom designed to accommodate new technology. A realistic alternative to static branch libraries would be a fleet of specialized vehicles—reference, multimedia, book— operating by microwave relay with a computer-based main library, as well as a cable television system. A fleet of vehicles operating singly or together, with backup, can conceivably provide a more comprehensive library service than current operations.

A Vehicle Fleet

I would also implement a "Community Access Vehicle," a van with VTR equipment and broadcast capability that would interface with existing cable tv networks. I would like to see something done with alter-

native energy systems. Solar energy offers many possibilities. Inner city vehicles may be solely electric in the future.

   DR: Describe the Berkeley telecommunications systems.

   EM: We use the Citizens Band radio system, which
is a low range, high density communications system.
It's an emergency system—that's why we have it.
It's impractical for use in a reference network, and
probably illegal. Remember, you're sharing a channel
with many thousands of people. Instead of being able
to get a message through, nine times out of ten you
wind up listening to somebody else.

   The Oakland vehicle, Operation
Outreach, used to be equipped with
radio-telephone. They used it once   Radio
or twice, over three years, at a   Communications
prohibitive monthly cost and final-
ly had it removed. Like CB radio,
radio-telephone is a crowded, over-
rated medium. CB radio is supposedly
designed for "relevant" communication, even though
it's continually violated. You're sharing these channels with a lot of people who have to find space to
squeeze in a quick message and that's about it. Reference questions are just not high priority on CB.
I personally think mobile link-up with a reference
base via microwave is the way it will go. UHF and
VHF frequencies are too tied up at present, unless
we want to share space with the fire department.

   Under current circumstances, with every department being cut for budget reasons, we have an incredible amount of resistance to new technology from
people who claim that every technology imposes a
greater workload on its users. Of course, it could
simultaneously relieve that workload, but there's
always the strain of having to learn how to use it.
We do have the telephone and I must say, I've never
had a reference question that could have been better
handled with a microwave relay system. The Berkeley
system is probably unique. We're pretty small and
frequently understaffed (so I'm told). The Media Machine is no longer an experiment by library standards. By becoming a regular operation it has lost
some of the aura attendant to less permanent institutions. I have remained with the project because

of the autonomy that is essential to this project,
as well as for growth experience and development.

I have had a considerable amount of mail from
other libraries, both in and out of California.
Most asked "how did you do it" and "how much did
it cost." Many asked for schematic diagrams, exact
measurements, etc. Some libraries sent personnel
to measure and photograph with an aim, I suppose,
to duplicating the Media Machine.

DR: What parting shots do you have?

EM: Go ahead and experiment. There isn't any
tried and true approach in mobile programming, despite what Gerstenslager and the California Library
Association say. (The CLA subcommittee on Extension
Services wants to have certain accepted criteria
for mobile units—dimensions, equipment, etc.) Ana-
lyze the environment, find out what's available,
what you can afford and how far you can go, and do
it. A popular mistake is to copy someone else's
success and wind up with a failure. What works in
Berkeley might not work in Stockton or Modesto, so
be alert. Be flexible, ready to shift gears, change
course, or jump ship.

DR: How much does it take to do it from scratch?

EM: You either do your own, buy somebody else's,
or do nothing. Ultimately, it doesn't matter if
you have access to some media wizard or not, because you've already decided in your mind which way
you're going. It takes a pretty stiff backbone and
incredible patience to wrestle a media mobile from
a library board. It's worth it.

Jim Roberts

"The librarian's dream of true information access can now, finally, come true. The components
can now be assembled that will be truly revolution-
ary in impact. The hurdle has been leaped; we are
now within a realm that is not only cost competitive
with the Gutenberg library, but provides for almost
unbelievable freedom of informational choice for
users."

Jim Roberts designed and built one of the first
media vehicles and produced a film about it. His

interest in vehicles goes back to his formal training in automotive design in Los Angeles.

DR: I want to know where you think things are going to go, especially regarding the power-to-weight
ratio. How can vehicles be more economical? How can
we get beyond some of the conventions we are locked
into?

JR: The media machines that have been built to
date have largely been based on a conventional truck
chassis that is interchangeable with all the utility
vehicles on the roads today. It consists of a ladder
frame that is high off the ground and a long drive
train that puts the motor up front and drive wheels
out back. There is a lot of dead weight, wasted
space, and a high center of gravity: in short, it's
nineteenth-century engineering. In the case of a
bookmobile, the medium is the message. If the medium
happens to be a chassis with these conventional pro-
portions, there is no hope of making a vehicle that
doesn't essentially have the layout of a Gerstenslager. What applies to the mechanical feature of the
chassis also applies to the technological features
of the media that are served on the machine; almost
inevitably, hardbound print dominates.

Modular is the key concept in the future for machines that will have the virtue of greater economy,
safety, and information circulation capabilities.
Chassis should be modular. In other words, in the
future, the utopian bookmobile should be a forward
control, front wheel drive configuration with a much
lighter chassis than is currently used and with removable modules on the back. This would serve two
purposes: it's an ideal chassis for a
delivery system in the conventional
mode, yet it also allows for drops of   Delivery
modular environmental boxes at insti-   System
tutions and other places. You not only
have a delivery system but you also
have the option of a drop environment
as well. There is no reason why those
two principles could not be applied
to a common drive train. There is no reason why
these modular boxes could not have quite exotic con-
figurations with increased application in areas of
specialized use. It's not merely an issue of where

media machines are going but where information envi-
ronments are going, what they will look like.
The adaptability of the boxes would be systemat-
ic. One box module would be suitable for video, another would be a mixed media affair involving lightweight materials for dissemination, like paperbacks.
There could be combinations for special service purposes and experimental modules where you could drop
a "book box" in a shopping center that would be operable without the benefit of the chassis being
around. That's the vehicle as I see it.

DR: What kind of savings do you predict this vehicle might realize in terms of fuel consumption?

JR: Fuel would be the major saving if you go with
lighter modern media, and if you select the right
gross vehicle weight chassis for the job. Don't impose the "hardbound overburden."

DR: Will we ever get away from the internal combustion engine or will that be around for a while?

JR: It'll probably be around for a while, but
that's no excuse for not adapting engineering principles that are current right now. Sure you ought to
be able to get an electric chassis that would inter-
change with regular chassis. Volkswagen is producing
a front wheel drive module now that they are going
to be adapting to the bus and pick-up truck format.
Ford is going to do likewise in this country in the
near future. These would be suitable. You could cut
in half the weight that is now going out on your typical bookmobile. This would increase information capacity and the vehicle's agility and adaptability.
You could certainly cut your road costs in half.
What I see is a new vehicle system
with cooperation at the county, state,
and city level. That would mean working   Standardized
an interagency circuit. It would re-   Vehicle
quire standardization so that you have   System
the capability of forming a centralized
vehicle pool that would be the essential box mover. The savings are there
because these are multiple service vehicles. You don't need to tie up a Gerstenslager bookmobile (warming up and cooling down) that is not
adaptable in any media modification. I think the
Berkeley machine is the most advanced machine on the

road because of its adaptability and light weight.
Still, it is only a slightly superior Gerstenslager
due to its basic "primeval" chassis engineering.
Once you free yourself from the limitations of that
chassis you can have a vehicle that needs not, in
order to provide a basic information environment,
exceed the overall length of a typical American station wagon, and with less overhang. Then you really
have something!

DR: In a state like New Mexico, where there are
such vast distances between places, would it make
sense to go to something in the future like helicopters, or is that too exotic?

JR: Helicopters are no good. Light airplanes are
a much more economical delivery system. Airplanes
cost about a quarter as much to run as a helicopter
and there are enough fields around for them to land
on.

DR: Would that work with this modular box system?

JR: Planes wouldn't carry the modular box, but
they would carry materials in software and hardware
out to the field. They could circulate video packs,
too, and other equipment with expensive down time.
The virtue of the 'copter would be that it could
carry the module. But where are you going to get the
money to run one? Best to have your modules circulated piggyback.
    See what I mean? As the demand arises in the com-
munity, it can be responded to on the WATS line and
within a week the space equipment can be sent out
via, say, a light plane.

DR: What other developments can you think of right
now that might be incorporated?

JR: Well, leaving interlibrary loan and computer
data and processing aside, I'm concentrating on dissemination and production.
    Video must be the way to go as a basic medium of
dissemination. It is the only medium that can satis-
factorily act as a synthesizer and disseminator of
all audiovisual material in one format. Video can do
this successfully. Films, filmstrips, local produc-
tions (which would probably be in the video medium
in any case), super-8, community resource materials
like slides, can all be programmed, added to, and

processed in the video format. Video provides the most standardized way of reaching the community: color TVs are already there in homes, for one thing. This particular literacy—or currency, if you like— of video in the community exists to a greater extent than for any other medium. Video is also cheaper.

DR: Cheaper than what?

JR: Cheaper than duplication of 16mm film, super-8 film, etc. You don't need to field any other dissemination equipment than video.

Afterthoughts

Without the transitional work done by the people interviewed in this Reporter, we would have little to learn from or critique. Their vehicles provide a bridge to the future of mobile service and a guide toward the standards of tomorrow.

The growing demand for media integration, spurred on by the use of sophisticated communications practices should lead, in the coming decades, to vehicles with a usefulness unknown in our time. But first vehicles must justify their existence in terms of energy priorities. What will happen when the library cannot afford gasoline for a vehicle that averages only one to five miles per gallon? We must begin now to look beyond the road and highway to see how we can achieve information mobility in totally new ways. We have barely considered, for example, the ways that railroads, ferryboats, and other public transportation systems can serve information needs.

Politics are becoming more and more important to media vehicle survival. We must put pressure on local and state legislatures, the Congress, the Interstate Commerce Commission (ICC) and the FCC to insure our place in a changing communications environment. Likewise, we must work with private corporations like International Telephone and Telegraph (ITT) and hardware producers to insure the advancement of our mutual interests. We must reject high developmental costs as an excuse for postponed improvements. We should collaborate with HEW and the vehicle manufacturers in securing research and development grants to improve vehicle design and construction.

If we want to reach beyond our own vehicles, we must investigate alternative approaches. We must challenge and advance vehicular design through direct involvement in design improvements and through encouraging engineers to initiate new solutions to our problems. We might sponsor library workshops on design, seek grants for a design institute, or encourage manufacturers to join us in establishing one.

If the library fails to take the initiative, it seems virtually certain that our mobile information services will be replaced by services sponsored by other public agencies or the private sector. We have much to learn from nonlibrary vehicles such as those built and operated by street video people, Civil Defense, cable TV companies, and others.

Libraries planning new units must look 15 to 20 years into the future. Since replacement costs are bound to soar, it is irresponsible to plan for, purchase, and operate obsolete vehicles. We must take risks to ensure that public libraries have mobile possibilities. This Reporter notes some novel suggestions such as "piggyback" setups with removable modular units that can be exchanged with a variety of service systems. Although modular design is initially more expensive, it increases the vehicle's possibilities and may prove more cost-effective in the long run. Interchangeability and expandability may be the key to mobile survival.

Are we important enough in the overall information picture to make a case for improved and continued library vehicular service? If not, how do we get there? We have the possibility of performing excellent on-the-spot reference work via radio-telephone; we can provide facsimile printouts; we can pick up satellite, microwave, and laser television transmissions; we can provide access to the material resources of surrounding regions through book or microfiche catalogs; we can produce sophisticated, remote production and playback of media. Only by providing such services can we establish the credibility we need for survival in the coming decades when knowledge transfer will be dominated by electronics.

If the library continues its print-dominated service—whether in buildings or bookmobiles—it will
have to settle for an archival, secondary status,
thus losing credibility with the taxpayer, the potential customer. By developing media mobile services,
we can encourage media integration, telecommunications activity, alternative energy development and
fuel economy, flexible scheduling, media production,
regional planning, and innovative programming and
information delivery.

Let's hope the mediamobile pioneers will be more
appreciated in the future, as their experience and
ability work for all of us. The year 2002 could see
vehicles that bear little or no resemblance to that
fledgling motorized library cart that rolled through
the streets of Maryland in 1902. But that future is
up to us.

Appendix
Media Vehicle Specifications

The following list consists of specifications
for mediamobiles supplied by major mediamobile manufacturers. For up-dated, state-of-the-art information, contact the libraries or the manufacturers
for further details.

<u>Portland (Maine) Public Library</u>

Chassis: International Harvester
Body: Thomas F. Maroney Co., Inc.
Year of manufacture: 1972
Body dimensions (l,w,h): 30' x 8' x 10½' (21' from
    back of driver's seat to rear inside panel)
Weight, loaded: 24,000 lbs.
Miles per gallon, loaded: 5.3
Auxiliary power plant: Kohler
Output: 7.5kw
Additional information: Two-way Motorola radio with
    main library as base station. Stereo music sys-
    tem with interior and exterior loudspeakers.
    Side-panel exterior movie screen with rear view
    projection. Air conditioning. Hydraulic life for
    wheelchairs and extra wide doors for handicapped.

Memphis-Shelby County (Tennessee) Public Library

Chassis: Chevrolet
Body: Gametime, Inc.
Year of manufacture: 1972
Wheelbase: 157"
Body dimensions (l,w,h): exterior--285½" x 94 7/8"
    x 131½"
    load area—192" x 93" x 84 7/8"
Weight, loaded: 10,350 lbs.
    unloaded: 9,050 lbs.
Miles per gallon, loaded: 11.4
    unloaded: 13
Auxiliary power plant: Kohler
Output: 7.5kw-220 volts
Additional information: Unit has a pull-down screen,
    built-in record changer, cassette deck, two ex-
    terior and two interior loud speakers, and is
    air conditioned.

Vigo County (Indiana) Public Library

Chassis: International Harvester
Body: Gerstenslager
Year of manufacture: 1975
Wheelbase: 217"
Body dimensions (l,w,h): 28'6" x 96" x 10'6"
Weight, loaded: 17,100 lbs.
    unloaded: 15,010 lbs.
Miles per gallon, loaded: 7
Auxiliary power plants: Kohler and Onan
Output: 10kw and 2.5kw, respectively
Additional information: Miles per gallon figure in-
    cludes the use of auxiliary power plant since
    there is only one gasoline tank.
Storage includes: 100' standard book shelving; 20'
    paperback shelving; 12' children's shelving;
    8' locker storage for projection screens; 4'
    plastic display shelving for magazines; 1' slid-
    ing bin storage for phonorecords; 20' locker
    shelving and drawer space for audiotape cas-
    settes, filmstrips, games, 8mm films, slides,
    viewmaster reels, and cassette recorders; film-
    strip/slide projectors, slide viewers, and view-
    masters. Videotape equipment, automatic slide
    projectors, 16mm films, and projectors carried as
    needed. Dial mobile telephone on radio telephone
    channel.

Daniel Boone Regional Library, Columbia, Missouri

Chassis: International Harvester
Body: Gerstenslager
Year of manufacture: 1973
Wheelbase: 168"
Body dimensions (l,h): 28' x 11'8"
Weight, unloaded: 27,860 lbs.
Miles per gallon, loaded: 4.5
Auxiliary power plant: Kohler
Output: 10kw

San Francisco Public Library

Chassis: Dodge P-400
Body: Gerstenslager P-500
Year of manufacture: 1970
Wheelbase: 154"
Body dimensions (l,w,h): 26' x 9.7' x (approx.) 11½'
Weight, loaded: 21,000 lbs.
Miles per gallon, loaded: 5
Auxiliary power plant: Onan generator
Output: 4kw-120 volts
Additional information: Special window on right side
    of body with plexiglass screen (36" x 24" x ¼")
    for viewing films on outside of vehicle. Hinged
    canopy. Equipped with 16mm Bell & Howell projec-
    tor, amplifier, Scott stereo AM/FM receiver,
    tape recorder, exterior speakers, and PA system.
    Fifty-one feet of shoreline cable for electrical
    hookup to utility poles or buildings.

Richmond (California) Public Library

Chassis: General Motors Corp.
Body: Boyertown
Year of manufacture: 1973
Wheelbase: 137"
Body dimensions (l,w,h): 21'1" x 6'10½" x (approx.)
    9'3"
Weight, loaded: 10,000 lbs.
Miles per gallon, loaded: 9
Auxiliary power plant: Kohler
Output: 4kw
Additional information: Automatic transmission, pow-
    er steering and brakes; exterior rear view pro-
    jection screen. The operator plans to add a 500/
    watt invertor because 4kw are not used and the
    present generator is noisy.

Berkeley (California) Public Library

Chassis: International Harvester MA 1200
Body: Wave Project
Year of manufacture: 1969
Wheelbase: 134"
Body dimensions (l,w,h): 11' x 78" x 7'
Weight, loaded: 7720-8000 lbs.
Miles per gallon, loaded: 10-14
Auxiliary power plant: McCullough
Output: 2kw

Mediamobile Bibliography

Prepared by George A. Plosker

Public and state libraries use mediamobiles, particularly in outreach programs to the rural poor and to institutions such as prisons and hospitals. School districts have purchased custom-tailored units to serve as instructional materials centers to serve locations without a permanent library. The business world is discovering the special purpose mediamobile as a source of technical information.

The literature available on media applications in bookmobiles published between 1964 and 1975 reaches several conclusions. When designing a bookmobile, cooperation between librarian and coachbuilder is a key to success. The major manufacturers of bookmobiles now offer custom design in order to provide a vehicle suited to the specific needs of any library. A more reliable product is also needed. Fifteen years ago, custom-designed vehicles incorporating the latest in information hardware were prophesied for the future. Today, custom-designed mediamobiles are widely used. In the future, more sophisticated mediamobiles will find even wider application.

A recent American Library Association convention provided additional information on this topic. Gerstenslager, perhaps the foremost manufacturer of bookmobiles, is emphasizing media applications in custom-designed units. Bro-Dart offers a custom-designed library trailer complete with books, media software, and all necessary media equipment.

"Bookmobilers' Maryland Meet. Reveals Wants and
    Needs." Library Journal 98:3491-2 (December 1,
    1973).
    Relates the important conclusions of the 3rd
Annual Conference of Bookmobilers, which was held
in 1973 at Hood College, Frederick, Maryland. Speak-
ing to seven manufacturers of bookmobiles, generators, and chassis, bookmobile librarians demanded
"a more reliable product." Suggested improvements
included: auxiliary lighting, adequate power
sources, automatic transmissions, improved door
closures, relocatable magazine shelving, and background music. The type of fuel used by bookmobiles
was also discussed, reflecting the librarians' concern with environmental pollution. Propane and diesel power were considered more efficient and clean-
er burning.
    Some library administrators still doubt the val-
ue of bookmobiles and two of these spoke to the
group. They charged that bookmobiles are inadequate
and unreliable. A suggested alternative was informal
branch libraries, without professional staff, located in shopping centers. Bookmobiles are proving most
useful and popular in institutional applications,
such as prisons and outreach programs.

Brown, Eleanor Francis. Bookmobiles and Bookmobile
    Service. Metuchen, N.J.: Scarecrow, 1967. 471p.
    The only single, comprehensive volume offering
bookmobile information in detail and depth. The book
covers all aspects of bookmobiling, including his-
tory, choosing the bookmobile, operating details including maintenance, standards and evaluation, cost
information, staff information, bookmobile specifications, and collections. There is an extensive bibliography, and 57 illustrations, including photos
of all types of bookmobiles. The book attempts to
assess strengths and weaknesses of bookmobiles in
relation to other library services. Extensive de-
tailed information of criteria for designing and
choosing a bookmobile is provided. In a listing of
bookmobile trends and prophecies the author stated:
        Specialized vehicles tailored for use as audio-
        visual centers, carrying books, phonograph re-
        cords, films, magazines, pamphlets, players,
        tapes and tape recorders, record players, pro-
        jection equipment, and portable TV will be de-

veloped and used more widely, both for public
library service and school service in consoli-
dated rural districts. Such a bookmobile now
serves the Choctaw Indian Schools in
Mississippi (p.39).

"Centennial College Library Resource Van." Ontario
Library Review 55:128 (June, 1972).
Centennial College serves approximately 80
square miles of eastern Toronto and currently offers
courses at eight locations. To provide library service at these locations a Volkswagen delivery van
has been converted into a bookmobile that can supply
instructional materials. Rolling stack shelving has
been installed so that the appropriate shelf can be
pulled out for display. Response from students has
been good and use of the van is increasing. The van
stocks books and audiovisual materials.

"Educational Mediamobile Serves Colorado School District." Library Journal 99:1174 (April 15, 1974).
This Educational Mediamobile (EMM) is a converted standard school bus, modified to serve as a
traveling classroom. Shelves, work counters, a projection screen, and electrical power sources were
built into the bus. The EMM contains approximately
425 titles of multimedia sources including 16mm
films, filmstrips, pictures, charts, color slides,
audio tapes, test kits, and other materials. The aim
of the project is to provide an environmental education center where both multimedia and multidisciplin-
ary materials can be supplied to motivate students
to understand environmental issues. A printed book
catalog of the multimedia sources was also developed
as part of the project. The catalog is made available to teachers in the district, and has facilitat-
ed and increased use of the EMM.

Goldstein, Harold. "Bookmobiles: Where Do We Stand
with Them Now?" Bowker Annual. New York: Bowker,
1964, p.98-100.
This 1964 article discusses the past, present,
and future role of bookmobiles. The author points
out that "in some library systems, the addition to
the bookmobile stock of nonprint materials is an innovation." In 1962 one unusual use of a bookmobile
was reported. The Illinois State Library used a
specially equipped vehicle to conduct a workshop in

library skills to nonprofessional staff in the
small libraries around the state. This vehicle was
equipped with a variety of visual and other aids,
lounge chairs, mechanical devices and demonstration
equipment. This example illustrates possible new
uses of mobile units. "There could be a different
kind of vehicle—or several—in the near future
which uses machinery (hardware) of amazing complex-
ity in library operations." The author feels that
these ideas are technically and financially within
reach of the profession.

————, issue editor. "Current Trends in Bookmobiles." Library Trends 9:285-384 (January, 1961).
    Although dated, this issue of Library Trends re-
mains one of the only comprehensive treatments of
bookmobiles and bookmobile service. Nine articles
discuss all aspects of bookmobile service. In "Selection of the Bookmobile," P. Wyer describes design
from both a technical and service viewpoint. Wyer
provides specific information on sizes and types of
bookmobiles, interior equipment (shelving, desks,
storage space, skylights, etc.), sources of electrical power, heating, air conditioning, chassis selection, and decoration. Maintenance of bookmobiles is
also treated.

Hanna, Mary Ann. "Media by Mobile." Wisconsin Library Bulletin 64:249-50 (July, 1968).
    In order to help teachers become aware of audio-
visual materials, the Michigan State Library purchased a Mediamobile for use with teacher in-service
programs. The mediamobile is a 35-foot truck-van,
equipped with motion picture, filmstrip, slide,
opaque and overhead projectors, a tape recorder, phonograph, and equipment to make transparencies. Display areas, made of various background materials,
work space for production of materials, and carrels
for individual viewing or listening, as well as
space for small groups to utilize the materials and
the equipment, are provided. The mediamobile contains
storage racks, shelves, and cabinets for books,
films, filmstrips, tapes, records, maps, and other
materials. Teachers meet with the audiovisual director for the district, tour the mediamobile, and see
demonstrations of varied enrichment resources. The
mediamobile has proven good for provision of in-
service training and has encouraged the wide, varied,
integrated use of media in the school curriculum.

Healy, Eugene. "Bookmobiles: A Somewhat Closer Look."
American Libraries 2:72-78 (January, 1971).
The author describes the problems experienced by
Jamestown (New York) with a new bookmobile and con-
cludes that a more reliable and sophisticated vehicle is needed. The problems included overweight, constant generator trouble, poor engineering and design,
and severe and recurring mechanical problems. Future
vehicle specifications are suggested: length 35 feet,
height 11 feet, gross weight not to exceed three-
fourths of the chassis rating; streamlined body, all-
metal frame, outer panels and doors; low profile
chassis to keep the interior floor near the ground;
air-cushioned suspension that is manually adjustable
on all four corners; a diesel engine, rear-mounted
to allow a shorter drive shaft; and a generator,
driven by the truck engine, providing power for heat,
light, air conditioning, photocharging, and auxilia-
ries. The author provides recommendations for shelving, floor coverings, toilet facilities, radio telephones, movies, music, portable photocopiers, framed
art prints, and driving accessories. The article
calls for establishment of standards for bookmobiles
and bookmobile service.

Moody, Joyce H. "IMC on Wheels." Library Journal
92:304-5 (January 15, 1967).
This article describes a special bookmobile program designed to provide an Instructional Media Center (IMC) facility to schools in a poverty-striken
area of California. The El Rancho Unified School District contracted the Crown Coach Corporation of Los
Angeles to build a special purpose bookmobile. The
cost was $33,525, approximately $10,000 more than
ordinary mobiles. This large, tailor-made unit is
35'x 8', with an interior space of 280 square feet.
It is fully air conditioned, heated with a three-fan
pump, and lit with fluorescent lights. In addition to
shelving for 5,000 volumes, there are adequate storage cabinets for instructional materials. All interior equipment was custom made under subcontracts from
the bus company. The mobile houses filmstrips, projectors, records, study prints, and magazines. Instead of tables and chairs, a thick, durable carpet
was laid so that students might sit on the floor for
library instruction and story hours. Thirty-five students can be accommodated aboard the mobile library
for instruction and browsing. Story hours, utilizing

recorded tapes or discs have proven very popular.
Filmstrip lessons have also worked out well. Crown
Coach provides full maintenance and service for the
unit. This is viewed as desirable.

Pennell, Lois G., ed. The Bookmobile--A New Look.
    Chicago: American Library Association, 1969. 61p.
    This book of nine articles by different authors
is a comprehensive look at bookmobile service. The
main objective of the bookmobile, "to bring the book
to the reader, to make a library's resources available to its public," is the book's focus. Converted
buses and trucks have proven unsatisfactory as bookmobiles; therefore, it is suggested that all bookmobiles be constructed by specialized, commercial
firms. The Louisiana State Library publishes a set
of sample specifications for a suggested bookmobile.
One article describes the controversy between electrical hookup to outside lines at bookmobile stops
and internal power source.
    The last essay is written by A. Baehr, a sales
manager of Gerstenslager Company. He feels that the
success of any bookmobile "will depend largely on
the degree of cooperation between the librarian who
plans its service facilities and the body builder
who designs its overall construction." The bulk of
Baehr's article is a technical discussion of color-
ing, styling, roof structure, service facilities,
air conditioning, heating, lighting, floor coverings,
and new uses of bookmobiles. The author states:

    As more school districts across the country
    accept full responsibility for libraries in
    their schools, a new market is being opened to
    bookmobile builders. New units are designed as
    school library materials centers and remedial
    reading laboratories. Audiovisual facilities
    are included with pull down projector screens
    permanently mounted in the ceiling. Sometimes
    carrels are built in for individual study.
    Other conveniences are being added for the use
    of teacher-librarians.

Pfoutz, Daniel R. "Penntap." Library Journal
    94:1589-91 (April 15, 1969).
    The Carnegie Library of Pittsburgh is utilizing
a "sci-tech mobile" to alert small industry to technical information via the Pennsylvania Technical
Assistance Program (Penntap). The vehicle visits

qualified institutions, library district centers, business firms, and industrial plants. The mobile is provided with a slide projector, periodical racks, photocopier, and chairs. Window shades may be drawn, and a projection screen dropped from the ceiling so that small groups may meet inside for discussions. The van carries about 2,000 books and 80 periodical titles.

"RAM VAN: New Multimedia Experiment of the Buffalo and Erie County Public Library." Library Journal 97:1858 (May 15, 1972).

The RAM Van (Readily Accessible Materials), a canopied van chock-full of the latest instructional materials and devices and working with existing educational and community groups in the inner city areas, is the new multimedia experiment of the Buffalo and Erie County Public Library. The van will accommodate between 20 and 25 persons for listening, reading, viewing, or discussing the books, magazines, films, tapes, and slides that it carries. The all-weather vehicle, which is air conditioned and heated, carries folding tables and chairs to make its interior as flexible as the programs require.

"TREES and FREDD." American Libraries 6:19-21 (January, 1975).

The Connecticut State Library for the Disabled has set up a program using a specially designed multimedia bookmobile. Called FREDD (Free Resources for Educating the Developmentally Disabled), the bookmobile is basically designed to demonstrate high-interest, low-vocabulary library materials for learning disabled adults and children with reading comprehension up to grade five. Materials exhibited include picture books; mystery stories; filmstrips and books on sex education, occupations, driving skills; weekly newspapers; cookbooks; and materials for parents of the learning disabled. A full-time librarian travels with the bookmobile to operate the audiovisual equipment, and answer questions of parents, school and public librarians, special education teachers, and convalescent home administrators.

"Vigo County Public Library Institutes Mediamobile Service." Focus on Indiana Libraries 26:82 (Summer, 1972).

Vigo County Public Library has instituted media-

mobile service to both urban and rural communities.
A modified bookmobile handling a full range of me-
dia--from printed matter to audiovisual materials--
and equipment to use it, a Sony Videorover back-pack
video tape recorder (VTR), is being used. The mediamobile provides year-round service to low income
areas in the county. The project attempts to encourage and train users to plan for themselves and
to develop their own educational programs. "Among
objectives of the program are demonstrations of the
potential of new forms of information and equipment
in the public library program. The project will en-
able disadvantaged residents to upgrade themselves
through a public library program that provides information resources and assistance in using the information."

Index

Compiled by Sanford Berman
Head Cataloger, Hennepin County Library
Edina, Minnesota